SALES TA...
HOLDING YOUR GROUND
AND PROTECTING YOUR PROFIT

CRUSH PRICE OBJECTIONS

TOM REILLY

New York   Chicago   San Francisco   Lisbon   London   Madrid   Mexico City
Milan   New Delhi   San Juan   Seoul   Singapore   Sydney   Toronto

The McGraw·Hill Companies

Library of Congress Cataloging-in-Publication Data

Reilly, Thomas P.
    Crush price objections : sales tactics for holding your ground and protecting your profit / by Tom
Reilly. —1st ed.
        p.   cm.
    ISBN: 978-0-07-166466-0 (alk. paper)
    1. Selling.   2. Sales management.   I. Title.

HF5438.25 R4   2010
658.85—dc22   2009031991

To Paul, my son,
a talented young salesman

1 2 3 4 5 6 7 8 9 10 11 12 13 14 15 16 17 18 19 20   WFR/WFR   1 9 8 7 6 5 4 3 2 1 0

ISBN 978-0-07-166466-0
MHID   0-07-166466-1

McGraw-Hill books are available at special quantity discounts to use as premiums and sales promotions or for use in corporate training programs. To contact a representative, please e-mail us at bulksales@ mcgraw-hill.com.

Contents

Preface

I Want to Help You Get Your Price

"Your price is too high."
"I can buy this cheaper somewhere else."
"Your competition offered us a better deal."
"My budget will not allow for this."
"I must send this out on bid."
"I just do not see your value."

Price resistance is universal. Whether you work in the service industry, manu-facturing, or distribution, you are invariably confronted with one or more of these statements as a price objection. Business-to-business and consumer sales-people alike face price resistance on a daily basis. If you are a salesperson, it will come as no surprise to you that price objections are the most common objection salespeople bring to our seminars.

The driving forces behind price objections are plentiful and diverse:

■ **The state of the economy—broadly and specifically.** We can sail along smoothly in one area of the economy and sink in another. Because of its cyclical nature, there is a natural ebb and flow. As economic growth slows, price resistance increases.

■ **Supply and demand.** When supply is greater than demand, buyers purchase less of the available supply, and prices drop.

■ **Ubiquitous price sellers.** In retail, wholesale clubs and big-box superstores have taken the super out of service and the value out of value-added reseller. Integrated supply, group purchasing organizations, and online reverse auctions drive prices down in the industrial selling market. For consumers, the Internet offers direct access to goods and savings.

■ **Pressure from manufacturers.** Manufacturers have capacity requirements, volume goals, and profit objectives. These add additional pressure to distributors.

■ **Bidding.** The current global obsession for bidding goods and services reduces the number of negotiated deals. The bid process accelerates during tough times, as suppliers may witness double or triple the number of competitors vying for a piece of business.

■ **Savvy buyers.** Thousands of seminars teach buyers how to chisel salespeople out of their margins. As you are reading this, your buyers are studying their resource materials on negotiating sharper deals.

■ **Buyer perception.** Advertisers tout "value," convincing buyers price is all that matters. This emphasis on price is turning *value* into a euphemism for *cheap*.

■ **Willingness of sales force to lower price.** My company, Tom Reilly Training, recently surveyed a mix of 125 industrial and construction salespeople to determine how many would discount for their top customer; 72 percent said they would discount if the customer asked for a cheaper price.

Separately, in a study of 1,769 salespeople and sales managers, 58 percent told us that they would cut price for their top customer. Even sales managers admitted their willingness to reduce prices.

There is nothing new about this problem. Salespeople have faced price issues for centuries. Art critic John Ruskin wrote, "There is hardly anything in the world that some man cannot make a little worse and sell a little cheaper, and the people who consider price only are this man's lawful prey." Ruskin died January 20, 1900.

The inevitability of price objections is a compelling reason for you to read this book, study the principles contained herein, and apply the concepts to your daily selling. If you are like most salespeople, you are frustrated and fed up. You worked hard for the business, and you are watching it slip through your fingers. You feel buyers have short memories or ignore all the good things you have done, as they obsess on price and overlook your value. You feel pressure from your manager. Your operations team and your suppliers are pushing for volume, and all of them want you to maintain your prices and protect your—and by extension, their margins. You resent the inequity of giving more than you are getting, which leads to feelings of resentment. You feel like the competition has targeted your customers specifically to launch a price war, and you are sitting at ground zero. You feel guilty fighting for a price when your customers are asking for your help or are suffering tough times. And you might feel you are gouging customers because you are making a profit. If you have found yourself in any of these situations, you are reading the right book.

My first book, *Value-Added Selling Techniques*, began as a response to price objections but immediately became the primer for a philosophy called *value-added selling*. Value-added selling has shaped sales cultures around the world since its first appearance on the global stage, and my work in this area remains the number one reason companies hire me to work with their salespeople. *Crush Price Objections* explores in depth one vital aspect of the value-added selling philosophy: price objections. It is the only book on the market that gives you the tactical support that you need to counter price resistance.

Crush Price Objections offers you relief on two levels. It builds both your confidence and your competence. When your confidence increases, your competence also increases. Imagine the impact on your closing ratio!

Reading this book will change your attitude forever, and you will no longer feel the need to apologize for your prices. You will avoid those embarrassing moments of silence when you do not know how to handle a price objection as it surfaces and never again be at a loss for something to say in the heat of a price battle. Here is your value proposition for *Crush Price Objections*: when you read this book and apply what you learn, you will be able to persist when buyers resist—holding the line on prices and protecting margins. You will find yourself more prepared to handle a price objection than the buyer is to offer it.

I have organized the book in four parts, each focusing on a different aspect of price resistance. Part I teaches you to think more like a businessperson when confronting price objections. You will learn

- the realities of selling in a price-sensitive market;
- factors that affect price sensitivity;
- the characteristics and types of price shoppers;
- what buyers really want from suppliers;
- the consequences of a price-selling philosophy;
- why salespeople cut price; and
- the important differences between price, cost, and value.

Studying the information in Part I will help you develop an in-depth understanding of the nature of price objections.

Part II provides strategies for avoiding price objections. Most people know the importance of being proactive. Once the toothpaste is out of the tube, it is difficult to replace it. The same concept applies to price objections. The best time to deal with them is *before* they become an issue. Avoiding price objections means being prepared to sell in a price-sensitive environment and achieving a preemptive selling advantage, which will help you assume early positive control of the sales conversation. Here are some key points covered in this section:

- The importance of personal preparation, collateral preparation, and call preparation
- How to ask questions that shift the focus off price
- How to change the conversation from price to broader and more important issues
- How to present your price in its best light

When you gain a preemptive selling advantage, you direct the conversation toward a buying decision that transcends acquisition price.

Part III is your guide to responding effectively to price objections. You are not helpless when the buyer rejects your price, so there is no reason to feel hopeless when confronted with this resistance. Being prepared to deal with price resistance does not mean making price objections a self-fulfilling prophecy. Whoever is better prepared for price negotiations—you or the customer—is more likely to emerge from that negotiation having won more negotiating points. Part III presents

- some general tips for dealing with objections;
- a four-step response model for engaging price objections;
- the five types of money objections; and
- forty-five ways to respond to price objections.

Studying, customizing, and rehearsing your responses to price objections is fundamental to building your confidence for winning the war on price resistance.

Protecting your margins is more than memorizing responses to buyer objections. Part IV shows you

- how to develop a discount discipline;
- why, how, and when to raise your prices; and
- how to bid—on paper and online.

Pricing discipline, a thorough understanding of price increases, and rethinking your bid strategy will help you retain maximum profit in the most challenging circumstances.

I wrote this book specifically for you. Begin by reading the chapter introduction, scanning the section headings, and reading the chapter summary. Now you are ready to read the chapter entirely. Take notes. Think of different selling situations that reflect the issues I discuss in this book. Having tested these ideas with tens of thousands of salespeople from different industries, I am confident that you will share their hope. The five most dreaded words in sales, "Your price is too high," need not be a deal killer. *Crush Price Objections* gives you the hope and information you need to deal successfully with this challenge.

Read with an open mind. If you find yourself thinking, "This will not work for me," reframe your thought as a question: "How can I make this work for me?" Remember, if you had all the answers for price objections, you would not be reading this. Use the ideas presented in this book, not the exact words. Make it sound like you. Integrate the concepts into your natural selling style. Commit to the hard work of crushing price objections.

Commitment is reflected in your passion and your willingness to work hard to achieve something. How committed are you to crushing price objections? Will you put up with some inconvenience along the way to minimize the impact of price objections? You already demonstrated a financial commitment by purchasing this book, but the full price of success includes the time and emotional investments you make to learn and apply these principles. You will discover that there are no shortcuts. William Makepeace Thackeray once said, "Life is a mirror." Life reflects what you put into it. A full commitment means full return on your investment; half the commitment, half the return; and no commitment, no results.

And while on the topic of commitment, I would like to acknowledge the generous and patient help of my wife, Charlotte, my chief proofreader. Her eagle eye is legendary. Linda, my assistant, always adds value to our work. I would also like to thank the staff at McGraw-Hill, Donya Dickerson, Tania Loghmani, Nancy Hall, and Rachel Chance, whose commitment to quality and excellence inspires all of us.

Good luck. Happy reading. I know you will enjoy the outcome.

PART I

YOU CAN BE A DRAGON SLAYER

According to legend, St. George saved the daughter of the king of Libya from the dragon that lived in the lake there. His cunning and bravery equipped him to overpower the beast and earn the dragon slayer title. Price resistance is a two-headed dragon: you lose if you cut price, and you lose if you do not cut price. If you cut price, you lose profit and brand presence. If you do not cut price, you risk losing the sale. Your battle with price may not be as dramatic as the legend of St. George, but it is, nevertheless, a real battle and one you can win. You can slay this two-headed beast.

You may be intimidated by price resistance because you do not understand it fully, making you feel powerless. This section prepares you for the battle by helping you understand the causes of price resistance and the nature of price shoppers. By reading Part I, taking notes, and studying these ideas, you learn to outwit and outmaneuver the dragon you battle—price resistance.

Facing Reality

Reality isn't the way you wish things to be, nor the way they appear to
be, but the way they actually are.
—ROBERT RINGER, *LOOKING OUT FOR #1*

Perception is subjective reality. It is the meaning that you attach to incoming
stimuli; what you see is reality for you. With price objections, your perceptions coupled with the buyer's perceptions may offer a discordant view of reality.
Resolving differences in your subjective realities is one of the fundamental challenges of dealing successfully with price objections. You may perceive your price
as fair while the buyer perceives it as unfair. The greater the divide between your
perceptions, the greater the challenge to resolve the price issue. You need to earn
a profit, and the buyer needs an equitable and viable solution.

This chapter is about bridging that great divide by introducing you to the
realities of price resistance. By studying these realities and integrating them
into your daily selling, you are invoking an objectivity that may prove to be
your greatest weapon when battling the beast of price resistance. Specifically,
this chapter will cover the following:

- Ten realities that shape the landscape of selling in a price-sensitive
  environment
- How your attitudes influence the outcome of your efforts

A key characteristic of resilient people is their willingness to face reality as it is, not as they wish it were. We begin with ten realities that affect your life as a salesperson. Accepting and integrating them into the context of your sales presentation provides the energy behind the death blow to the beast.

REALITY #1: YOU WILL HEAR PRICE OBJECTIONS

They go with the territory. In spite of your best efforts, someone will object to your price. As a consumer, do you accept the first price a salesperson presents to you? No, of course not. Think about your last major purchase—house, appliance, or vehicle. Did you attempt to negotiate a better price? When you were a child, did you attempt to negotiate a bigger allowance? Have you ever negotiated your salary or compensation package? We wonder why buyers ask for a cheaper price, but facing price resistance is a sign that you are engaged in your territory.

REALITY #2: YOU WILL LOSE BUSINESS BECAUSE OF PRICE

There is some business you want to lose because of price. If you want competitors to have low-profit, high-aggravation, and slow-pay business, then take Napoleon's advice, "Never interrupt an enemy when he is making a mistake." From our research, we have concluded that if you are not losing one in six deals on price, your price is too low. If you target all customers as viable opportunities, you will mix price shoppers with value-added shoppers. With price-shopping customers, your in-pocket profitability is lower because they demand the same high level of treatment at a lower price. These two questions help you clarify your focus and face the reality of where to invest your sales time:

- ▪ Do you want every order or every opportunity?
- ▪ Have you ever met a customer whose business you did not want?

REALITY #3: YOU WILL SELL IN SPITE OF YOUR PRICE

In every seminar I have ever conducted, salespeople have told me, "I was able to sell for some reason other than a cheap price." Think about your own selling. Consider the last good or service you sold for which your price was higher than a competitor's and you still got the business. Why were you successful? Was it your service, product availability, or your relationship with the buyer? The customer recognized the value in your proposition and was willing to pay for it. Customers have taught you how to sell your total solution—in our terms, your value-added. Are you listening?

REALITY #4: EVERYONE WANTS EQUITY

When the buyer says your price is too high, he is more focused on what he is giving than what he is getting. When the buyer obsesses on price, he is locked in on his sacrifices more than your solution's advantages—his pain versus gain. The one thing the buyer wants more than a cheap price is equity. He wants to feel that he is getting at least as good as he is giving. The sale is always about the customer, and his perception of value is sacrosanct.

Drawing from management psychology, equity theory explains employee-motivated behavior. People want equity from their work; they want a fair return on their personal investment. If they perceive equity—getting as good as they are giving—they are motivated to perform. The same concept applies to buying behavior. People buy when they feel they get as good as they give. Your task is to present your solution as an equitable exchange for the buyer's money. Here is a paradox: equity exists in the buyer's mind, not in your mind. It is not reality unless the customer views it as reality.

REALITY #5: SOME PRICE OBJECTIONS ARE FAKE

Some price objections are real; some are not. Fake means that price is not the real reason the buyer is hesitating. Whether the resistance is real or a red herring, there is an incentive for the buyer to bargain on price. If the buyer gets a better price, she wins. If not, she has lost nothing. From the buyer's perspective, why not ask for a lower price? Regardless of the motivation, you are dealing with a price issue at that moment.

REALITY #6: PREPARATION BUILDS CONFIDENCE

Whoever is better prepared for a price negotiation tends to emerge from that negotiation with a more desirable outcome. Being prepared does not guarantee your success, but being unprepared portends failure. Just as you never want to be out-prepared by the competition for a presentation, you never want to be out-prepared by the customer for a price negotiation. It is the one thing you control, and it affects your confidence and competence. Do you remember the one school test you studied for weeks in advance? This type of preparation fuels your passion and excitement, and this type of energy makes you persuasive and your argument compelling.

REALITY #7: YOU ARE SUPPOSED TO MAKE MONEY

Your company is in business to make a profit. Unless your company is a non-profit organization, you must earn a profit on a sale. You lose money when you discount. I have met salespeople who sold as if they worked for a nonprofit. For them, making a sale was more important than making a profit. The purpose of a business is to make money—hopefully, lots of it. There is no reason to feel guilty about making a profit. That is why your company is in business.

Profit is not a dirty word; it is the lifeblood of your company's ability to reinvest in its future. Profit funds your R&D, recruitment of top talent, and service programs. How can you deliver maximum value if you have nothing to give? The profit you garner in the form of a higher price is an investment your buyer makes in receiving greater value from your company in the future.

REALITY #8: SALESPEOPLE CREATE THEIR OWN MISERY

Most price resistance is a self-inflicted wound. Salespeople have taught buyers to object to price. A fifteen-year study of sales behavior conducted by the Vass Company appearing in a 1996 issue of *The Competitive Advantage* magazine reported that 90 percent of salespeople impulsively—and unprompted by buyer price resistance—offered a cheaper price to get the business. Salespeople are more tenuous about price than buyers. Researchers Peter Dickson, Florida International University, and Alan Sawyer, University of Florida, discovered that fewer than half of customers surveyed could name the price of a given product and that most customers underestimated the price. Could it be that the root of most price objections is buyers' lack of information about the price-determination process, resulting in expectations of a too-low price? Unrealistic expectations coupled with a lack of salesperson preparation guarantee price resistance and concessions.

REALITY #9: VOLUME IS NO SUBSTITUTE FOR PROFIT

An argument I often hear is, "I'll cut the price and make it up in volume." There is no guarantee you will make it up in volume. On the contrary, you could be multiplying your losses.

Several years ago, I was speaking to a group of salespeople. The president of the company introduced me to his group: "Ladies and gentlemen, we have some good news and some bad news. The bad news is, discounting has become horrendous in our industry, and our profit margins have plummeted to the point that we are now selling at ninety-seven cents on the dollar. The good news is, sales are down this year, so we are not losing as much money as we could be." The group laughed, and it set the stage for my presentation on value-added selling.

Most salespeople still believe they can reduce price and make up for it in volume. Can you? Do you want to? Do you really want more low-margin business? To paraphrase Warren Buffett, one of the smartest people in the world about money, when you're in a hole, stop digging.

REALITY #10: ATTITUDE DRIVES BEHAVIOR

People behave as they believe. They move in the direction of their thoughts and become what they think about. Once an attitude is in place, certain behavior naturally follows. This is the essence of the self-fulfilling prophecy: someone believes in outcomes and behaves in ways that create the outcomes he or she expects.

Your attitude about price affects price negotiations. If you enter a negotiation expecting price to be an issue, it will be an issue. Unwittingly, you will create a price objection. If you believe that factors other than price should be considered in a negotiation, likewise, you will create that outcome. Your attitude about price makes your expectations reality. If you enter a negotiation believing your price is too high, it will be too high. If you enter a negotiation believing you offer an incredible bargain, you will discover most people share your enthusiasm for the value of your solution. Your attitude influences the outcome.

Here are some negative attitudes about price that I have heard over the years from salespeople:

"Price is the only feature that sells in our industry."
"The only incentive buyers really care about is a cheap price."
"The only way to compete in our market is to have the absolute lowest price."
"It's a waste of time to convince someone to pay more for something."
"Forget service and support, what really counts is a cheap price."
"Hey, if I don't cut the price, I'll lose the business."

"It takes too much effort to avoid price objections."
"It's different in my industry; you can't sell value-added."

If you find yourself believing any of these self-defeating statements, you live and die by price objections. The remedy is simple: flush these ideas from your mind. Remove them from your thoughts and your beliefs. Expunge the negativism before it becomes your sales philosophy. These negative attitudes are like a disease that eats away at your spirit, hope, and effectiveness. Replace them with more positive, self-enhancing thoughts. Here are some examples:

"There are buyers who will pay more for a better solution. I have witnessed this in the past. I have seen these buyers. I have sold to them. I know who they are."
"Price is only one of several variables that go into the decision process. There are many factors that affect the buyer's decision to buy."
"My attitude about price affects my profit margins and my success."
"We sell something special, and I am excited about what we can do for the buyer."
"No product is overpriced unless it is under-desired by the buyer."
"The more value I build in on the front end, the less important price becomes on the back end."

Which set of attitudes, positive or negative, do you feel better prepares the salesperson to negotiate price more confidently? Which set of attitudes, positive or negative, do you think results in higher margins?

Some resistance to this concept is a strong indicator of the degree to which your attitude is holding you back. It is like driving with one foot on the brake and one foot on the gas. If you want to move forward, you will need to get your foot off the brake. Changing your attitude will accomplish this.

If you find it difficult to get excited about your product, service, or company, I suggest three alternatives. One, you need training. Learn more about your product. Study the impact your product has on the buyer. Review success stories and reignite the passion you once felt for your company and your product. Two, get another job. If you cannot get excited about what you sell, you are selling the wrong product. It is unfair to your employer, to your buyer, and mostly to you. On the other hand, if you are starting to feel some hope and getting excited, that is exactly where you ought to be at this point. Three, study this book like your future sales success depends on it—it does.

CHAPTER SUMMARY

Buyers and sellers have their own perceptions of reality. When your view of reality mirrors the buyer's reality, your job is easier. There are also a number of objective realities you must accept to succeed in sales. Your understanding of these realities and your attitude about price affect the outcome of your sales efforts. If you believe price will dominate the sale, it will. If you believe it will play a minor role, it will. In either case, you are right because you are creating a self-fulfilling prophecy. Since the outcome is strongly tied to your expectations, it is good strategy to have positive expectations.

2

Factors That Affect Price Sensitivity

Living is a constant process of deciding what we are going to do.
—JOSÉ ORTEGA Y GASSET, TWENTIETH-CENTURY SPANISH PHILOSOPHER

Decisions. Life is filled with them. Even a nondecision is a decision; it is a decision to do nothing. A buying decision is like any other decision a person makes. There are myriad influences on buying decisions, which makes it difficult to guess what is in another person's heart and head. Second-guessing human motivation has been the vocation and avocation of psychologists and philosophers for centuries. For the rest of us, studying the context in which people make decisions can offer clues about the motivation behind their decisions.

This chapter is about understanding the forces that influence price sensitivity. Your understanding of these dynamic forces and their impact on the buying decision provides context for you to frame your message of value. Specifically, in this chapter, you will learn about

- price elasticity and price sensitivity;
- factors that influence buyer price sensitivity; and
- buyer pressure points that mitigate the importance of price in buying decisions.

Although some buyers automatically reject price and value-strip your product, we will study buying decisions as a more sophisticated process than knee-jerk reactions to your price.

PRICE ELASTICITY AND PRICE SENSITIVITY

Prices increase; demand plummets. Prices increase; demand is stable. What to do? This is a sales book, not a primer on pricing strategy and tactics. For a more technical guide to price elasticity, I suggest reading any good economics book on the topic of pricing. Simply put, price elasticity describes the relationship between demand and price. Products are considered *elastic* if demand changes as prices change and *inelastic* if demand remains stable as prices change. Buyer *needs* tend to be inelastic, and buyer *wants* elastic. For example, people need fuel for their vehicles, and demand changes gradually as price increases. Fuel is an inelastic product. Premium or boutique coffees are more elastic. If Starbucks raises the price on a cup of coffee, demand falls because this product is more elastic. A cup of premium coffee is more *want* than *need*.

For our purposes, price sensitivity is the buyer's tendency to focus more (or less) on acquisition price for a variety of reasons. Understanding these driving forces makes you a more informed businessperson, better able to construct a compelling defense of your price.

FACTORS THAT AFFECT PRICE SENSITIVITY

Imagine the negotiating advantage you would have if you could peek inside the buyer's head to see how and why he makes decisions. As you read this, neuroscientists are doing that with functional MRIs, giving birth to an emerging field called neuromarketing. For now, unless you are a neuroscientist, you must rely on other clues to discern buyer motivation. Since people make relative-value decisions—weighing what they want to acquire against what they sacrifice to acquire it—it is important to understand the context in which they make their buying decisions. Some contextual factors increase price sensitivity, and others decrease it. Some create a mental tug-of-war for the buyer.

Factors That Decrease Price Sensitivity

Customer satisfaction, brand loyalty, and customer retention are inversely related to price sensitivity. This means that satisfied, loyal, and returning customers are less focused on price. They understand your value and appreciate it. With them, you have earned the right not to be the cheapest. This applies to your competition, too. If you are attempting to dislodge a competitor from a customer who is satisfied and loyal, you have a challenge ahead of you. Buyers change when the pain is greater than the gain.

Relationships mitigate the importance of price. The stronger the relationship, the bond the seller enjoys with the buyer, the less important price is. When two people trust each other and desire to do business with each other, they work out the details, and price is a detail. This is why some large companies attempt to set up a firewall between buyer and seller. They may use purchasing groups or outside consultants to prevent their buyers from becoming too close to the suppliers. They realize that when buyers and sellers have a special bond and feel a personal loyalty to a brand or salesperson, price becomes less of an issue. Selling is relationship management.

Engaged customers who participate in the sale and know more about your product are less price sensitive. They understand how your product's features and benefits apply to them. They use their knowledge to see advantages of which you may be unaware. Buyer engagement is key in a price-sensitive sale. Questioning and interactive presentations involve buyers. Think of ways you can engage your buyer.

There is an inverse relationship between price sensitivity and the gravity of the purchase. The more critical the decision, the less important price is. How many people price shop for heart surgery? How many people price shop child safety? Most people realize these are not the places to skimp. For critical purchases, risk associated with a cheaper price is a risk people want to avoid. This means you must establish a vital link between your product and the critical outcome the buyer wants and needs.

Closely related to the critical nature of the purchase is sunk-cost investment. This sunk-cost investment is the money buyers have already spent and will not recover. When buyers are heavily invested in a solution, they are less price sensitive for replacement parts, components, or upgrades. When your company is standardized on software, it will pay the upgrade charge for software enhancements because of the initial investment. Cost overruns are a close cousin to upgrades or enhancements. They are viewed as a business reality. Additionally, when customers share the cost of components or manufacturing with another company, they are less price sensitive because they are not paying for the total cost.

There is also an inverse relationship between price sensitivity and your ability to provide smaller shipments and hold inventory for customers. When the buyer can use your warehouse instead of her own and leverage those inventory dollars somewhere else, price is less of an issue. Their cost of capital—inventory dollars in this case—is likely higher than the price difference between you and the competition. Also, buyers are less price sensitive when they use a total cost of ownership analysis and appreciate the gain from your solution. Total cost of ownership refers to the initial price and ongoing costs buyers incur with a product or service. I offer a more detailed explanation of this concept in Chapter 6.

Customers who compete as a differentiator in their industries are less price sensitive. When your product or service adds to their differentiation, price is a moot issue. They leverage this difference into greater profitability in their market. Synergy is a powerful motivator to purchase and partner.

Factors That Increase Price Sensitivity

People are more price sensitive when spending their own money versus their company's money. Company money lacks the emotional connection of personal funds. People spend less and are more price sensitive when they use cash versus credit, which is one reason stores want you to use credit cards. You will spend more if you pay for it with plastic. It is similar to using chips in a casino; they do not have the same perceived value as cash. Credit is intangible; cash is tangible. This is why companies offer financing options.

Buyers are more price sensitive when they have information about buying alternatives. Choices allow them to make spreadsheet decisions. You can influence the decision if you invest time by sharing favorable information about your solution with customers. The more the buyer knows about your solution, the more ways you can distinguish yourself from the competition. Otherwise, the buyer value-strips your product and reduces it to its naked, commodity status. This is the most basic function that a product performs.

Price sensitivity increases with the size of the order. On large, big-ticket sales, buyers study price more closely. This is especially true for high-visibility purchases. For a smaller sale with less money involved, buyers feel their time is better spent in ways other than haggling over price.

Tug-of-War Factors

Some factors create a mental tug-of-war for the buyer. *Needs* and *wants* fall into this category. Buyers are less price sensitive for the niceties of life and more price sensitive for necessities of life. When it is a commodity sale—a transaction that is reduced to the value-stripped, naked product—the buyer is more price sensitive. If it is something they *need* versus something they *want*, they are more price sensitive. When was the last time you heard someone complain about the price of a new Mercedes? People *need* transportation, but they may *want* a luxury car. People complain about the cost of energy and food because they need both. When people *want* something, they figure out a way to buy it. *Wanting* is a powerful motivator. If you tap into the buyer's *wants*, price is less of an obstacle.

Before you pick up the phone to call me or fire off an e-mail, let me acknowledge the paradoxical relationship between sensitivity and elasticity. Earlier, I stated that demand remains stable for needs, even as prices change. Demand may remain stable because the buyer must have the product, but that does not mean the buyer will not shop the price. Gasoline for your car is the perfect example of that. You need first to run your car, but you may price-shop the lowest cost per gallon. High-end products may experience less demand, but those who want them really want them and will pay the price.

PRESSURE POINTS

Pressure affects price sensitivity. In negotiating, whoever feels the most pressure makes the most concessions. More pressure means price is less important. A pressure point is any condition that mitigates the importance of price. These pressure points displace price as the most important decision variable. If you feel more pressure to sell than the buyer feels to buy, you will make more concessions. Conversely, if the buyer feels more pressure to buy than you do to sell, she will make more concessions.

Note that the first item on the list of buyer pressure points provided in this chapter is timing. Have you ever noticed that when someone is in a hurry to purchase something, price is less important? A cheap price is meaningless when the buyer cannot get the product. Another pressure point is a bad experience with the competition. When someone has a negative experience with your competitor's product, your price is less of an issue. The more pressure points operating in a sale, the less likely the buyer is to fixate on price. Here are some tips on how to use buyer pressure points:

- During your sales call, turn on your sales radar and ask questions to expose the pressure points.
- Once you have determined which pressure points apply, send a follow-up letter (after the sales call) to recap and spotlight these pressure points.

Your strategy is to keep these pressure points top-of-mind with the buyer because they overshadow price.

■ Weave these pressure points into the summary of needs in your proposal. This is the first part of any proposal. It focuses the conversation and makes pressure points part of the buyer's total needs. When your buyer acknowledges pressure points at the beginning of your proposal, it sets the right tone to avoid price issues.

■ Use pressure points to respond to a price objection. In Chapter 15, there is a technique for responding to price objections called "the risk of cheapness." Assuming timing is the dominant pressure point the buyer is feeling, your response to a price objection might sound like, "Which offers you a greater risk at this point, paying more than you anticipated on the front end or not getting the availability you need on the back end to meet your timeline?" This pressure point is a strong counterpoint.

Buyer Pressure Points

■ Timing or the urgency to act is pushing the buyer.
■ There is a unique problem in the buyer's world.
■ There is a brand preference for your product.
■ There is a supplier preference for your company.
■ This decision is critical to the buyer's business.
■ Availability of supply favors you.
■ Your company offers a unique solution.
■ Many buyers are competing for your time.
■ The buyer had a bad experience with your competition.
■ There are few perceived substitutes for your product.
■ It is a painless transition to your solution.
■ The budget is available.
■ A budget deadline is closing in.
■ The buyer's business is doing well.
■ There are compliance issues (OSHA, EPA, etc.).
■ Your location is better for the buyer.
■ Appearing cheap impacts the buyer's image negatively.
■ The buyer's credit status is questionable.

■ Use this list of pressure points to make better seller decisions by reviewing it before making a decision to cut your price. If a buyer requests a lower price, refer to your "pressure point checklist." The more of these pressure points operating in this situation, the less likely you should be to cut the price.

CHAPTER SUMMARY

Understanding a buyer's decision-making process is crucial to your sales success. Buyers make relative-value purchasing decisions within the context of influencing forces. Price is only one of these influencers. Some products are elastic, and demand for them changes with price. Other products are more inelastic, and demand for them is stable even with price fluctuations. The driving forces behind price sensitivity offer you insight into why buyers focus more or less on price. Pressure points deflect or mitigate the importance of acquisition price. Your understanding of these forces and pressure points emboldens you and provides context for your presentation. Studying these forces will help you make better seller decisions.

3

Price Shoppers

Rommel, you magnificent bastard, I read your book.
—GEORGE C. SCOTT AS GENERAL GEORGE S. PATTON

In the movie *Patton*, George C. Scott, playing the role of General Patton, stood on a hilltop after his forces scored a victory over the enemy and crowed this often-quoted declaration. He was referring to a book, *Infantry Attacks*, written by his opponent, Erwin Rommel, known as the Desert Fox.

Knowing one's opponent is essential to victory. How combative this must sound to you! Buying and selling is not combat, and that metaphor is a turnoff for most people. It should be. Your job is not to battle the customer but to battle price resistance. Unfortunately, price resistance is personified in the buyer. A more positive view is that you are fighting for your profitability, not against your customer. Understanding price-shopping decision making equips you for the battle for your margins.

This chapter is about understanding price shoppers. Your knowledge of who they are and why they make price-oriented decisions puts you on that hilltop with Patton. To that end, here are the key points covered in this chapter:

- Four key characteristics of price shoppers
- Six types of price shoppers

The battleground for this fight is in the buyer's mind. The enemy is the price-shopping thought process, not the customer.

CHARACTERISTICS OF PRICE SHOPPERS

Price shoppers share some common denominators. These harbingers of what to expect from price shoppers make your job easier in deciding if you want to sell to them.

1. Time plays a major role in price shoppers' buying behavior. Typically, they have more time than money. Since they believe time is abundant and money scarce, they value money more than time and use time to gain money. On the other hand, when buyers have more money than time, they do not shop price as aggressively. When they have more time than money, they shop price.

Time also plays a dominant role in the price shopper's life, as they tend to be short-term thinkers. They operate in the here and now, which means they lock in on purchase price and lock out long-term gain. They are obsessed with acquisition price, not ownership or usage cost. To them, money is the bottom line on an invoice, not gain on a profit and loss (P&L) statement. Because of this short-term time horizon, price shoppers conveniently forget the favors you have done for them in the past. These favors are irrelevant because they are in the past. Because of this short-term thinking, price shoppers do not consider how you will take care of them in the future. That they live in the here and now suggests a strategy for working with them. This is covered in depth later.

2. Price shoppers wring you out and string you out. They will likely squeeze you on the front end for a cheaper price and pay late. To identify your most notorious price shoppers, ask accounts receivable. They will tell you by looking at how long it takes someone to pay. This caveat should prompt a discussion in your negotiation with the buyer to preempt late payments. If the buyer asks early in the discussions about your terms and late fees, run for the door.

3. The aggravation factor in dealing with price shoppers is high. They chew away at your bottom line like a school of profit piranhas. They have an insatiable appetite for concessions. They want a deal. Then, they return goods more often. They complain more. They have more requests. And, as just mentioned, they pay late. They will continue to nibble away at your profitability until you shut down the process. A great rule of thumb for the nibbler is to match his request for a concession with your own request for a concession—a tit-for-tat response.

4. **Price shoppers have a transaction mentality.** Because they are locked in on the here and now, their focus is the transaction. Value-added shoppers look beyond the transaction to the value of the relationship. Transaction shoppers go from deal to deal, much like order-taking salespeople. Their focus is on the immediate order. Transaction-based shopping behavior signals that price will dominate the decision process.

TYPES OF PRICE SHOPPERS

They come in all shapes and sizes. Some are motivated by need, and others are motivated by greed. Some price shoppers make price decisions because they are cheap; others shop price because they lack money. Some buyers view it as their job to shop price, and some make price decisions because they lack information. Understanding the type of price shopper you are selling to helps you maintain your sanity and your margins. Buyers who fixate on price represent an opportunity for you. They are begging for information on how to make a better buying decision. Sometimes they are unaware that they need this information. Emerging research gives us insight into some of these price-conscious shoppers. See how many of your customers you recognize here.

Bargain Hunters

These price shoppers buy because it is cheap. They find it difficult to pass up a sale sign. Every Saturday morning across America, bargain hunters go from one garage sale to another looking for the one thing they cannot pass up, a cheap price. They love "the deal." When you are cleaning out the warehouse to make room for new products, bargain hunters can be part of your cleaning crew. They will help you dispose of items you want to clear out. Just make them a deal too good to pass up. Present these sales as buying opportunities to avoid damage to your brand or credibility.

Cherry Pickers

They go from store to store, supplier to supplier, selecting the cheapest goods for their shopping lists. They may submit a request for pricing and buy only those items you offer at the cheapest price. They do this with all their suppliers. If you are the primary source for a cherry picker, you have a fighting chance to maintain your profitability. If you are the secondary or tertiary supplier and allow buyers to cherry pick, you end up selling only the low-profit items. One strategy for selling profitably to cherry pickers is to bundle your products and services as a packaged price. This prevents them from "spreadsheeting" your quote.

Tightfisted Shoppers

They hate to part with their money. It is painful for them to spend money, literally: brain-imaging research has demonstrated that the pain centers in their brains light up when they spend money. It does not matter what they are buying. This means you have a challenge on your hands if you are selling to a tightfisted shopper. Your struggle is to uncurl one finger at a time from around their money. Tightfisted shoppers procrastinate because it delays their spending. Ironically, these delays often cost the buyer more money, and this is a fact he or she must be encouraged to consider.

Savers

These customers enjoy saving money. It feels right to them. Brain imaging reveals that the pleasure centers in their brains light up when they save money. It is not that they hate spending money; they find saving money pleasurable. This suggests that you should adopt a strategy to demonstrate how investing money in your solution will save them money. Listen to the subtle cues that buyers send you about saving money.

Predatory Price Shoppers

These are especially pernicious buyers. Consumer studies estimate that they represent 10 percent of the buying public. They lie, cheat, steal, and engage in a host of other unethical practices to drive down prices. These predatory exercises are manipulative and create an adversarial atmosphere:

- Showing you a competitor's bid
- Requesting a last look at a quote
- Taking 2 percent terms for early payment and paying you late
- Lying about supply alternatives or using phony data in a negotiation

Do not be seduced into believing that any of this is sharp negotiating. This isn't sharp negotiating—it is lying! And lying automatically places a buyer into this category. Why would you want to reinforce this behavior? Why would you want to do business with this type of buyer? What is a salesperson to do? Be aware and beware of the price shopper to whom you sell. Then, decide how and if you will sell to them.

Gamesmen

Buyers in this category love the sport of negotiating. For them, it is a competition. This "win-lose" attitude is antithetical to the value-added selling philosophy, albeit a reality. Your willingness to participate in this competition determines your strategy. From my perspective, beginning a negotiation with the expectation of a win-win outcome eliminates the need for games.

CHAPTER SUMMARY

Price shoppers tend to share four common characteristics: a short-term viewpoint, problems with payment schedules, the aggravation factor of dealing with them, and a transaction mentality. The first question to ask is, knowing what we know, do we want to do business with price shoppers? We examined six different types of price shoppers, some motivated by need and others motivated by greed. Knowing which type of price shopper you are dealing with helps you develop your strategy. Some may require help with financing, some may need more information, while others may need reassurance that it is OK to spend more money than they had anticipated.

Buyers Want More than a Cheap Price

4

The heart deceives, because it is never anything but the expression of the mind's miscalculations.
—MARQUIS DE SADE, FRENCH ARISTOCRAT, REVOLUTIONARY, AND WRITER

A major mistake salespeople make is believing that price is all that matters. They hear this often from customers and take it to heart. Sometimes, the heart deceives. Once the deception is rooted, the self-fulfilling prophecy grows. Salespeople begin sales calls *knowing* price will be an issue, and voilà, price is an issue! What if your expectations are wrong? What if customers want something more than a cheap price? Is your heart deceiving you because you have miscalculated the buyer's needs and wants?

This chapter is about self-deception and reality. Once you realize how you and other salespeople have deceived yourselves into believing price is all that matters, you can begin to understand fully what the buyer needs and wants in a solution. Here are the major points covered in this chapter:

- How salespeople create their own misery when it comes to price
- What buyers really want in a solution

This information will challenge some of your most fundamental beliefs about buyers' priorities and put an end to the self-deception that causes you to cave in to price resistance.

PRICE OBJECTIONS ARE SELF-INFLICTED WOUNDS

Should salespeople have pricing authority? Few questions evoke the kind of passion that this one does. When I write opinion articles on this question, I can expect plenty of input from readers. My position is straightforward: Pricing is a strategic marketing decision. Pricing is a pillar of brand image. When this pillar is damaged, the whole edifice is disfigured.

My opinion does not come lightly to me. I have thought and argued about this for years. Salespeople should not have pricing authority. As a sales trainer, I know that most price objections are self-inflicted wounds. Consider the following information. In our ten-year (1995–2005) longitudinal study of buyers and sellers, we asked salespeople the same question that we asked buyers. On a 10-point scale with 10 as most important, how important is price? Salespeople rated price 8.3. Buyers rated it 6.9. Why the difference? It is simple: salespeople make a bigger deal out of price than buyers do.

A sales rep told me that he and his wife were shopping for a new home. They saw one they particularly liked and talked to the listing agent. She said, "Thank you for calling on this. I happen to know my seller is flexible on this price." She offered a price concession before the perspective buyer commented on the listing price. The agent led with the price. How would you like that salesperson working for you? She was not working for the seller but for the commission. A real estate sales manager once told me in a seminar that he tells his prospective clients that his fee is negotiable. He offers this concession before he gets a price objection! I think we should rename this phenomenon *pre-cession* to illustrate how ridiculous it is to offer a price reduction before engaging an objection.

We surveyed purchasing agents and asked, "Of the salespeople with whom you deal, what percentage of them will discount if you object to price?" They told us that about 75 percent of salespeople cut price when the buyer raises a price objection.

I collect antique fountain pens. I was in San Francisco on business and saw a particularly unusual fountain pen in the display case and asked the attendant, "How much is that?" Surprised by the price, I responded, "You're mighty proud of that."

He said, "I'm prepared to give you a 10 percent discount if you buy today."

I replied, "That's generous, but it's still a bit rich for me."

"Fifteen percent is as high as I can go on this item," he countered. Without breaking a sweat, I got him to reduce the price by 15 percent. No doubt that he was one of the three out of four salespeople who cave in when the buyer says, "Your price is too high."

One day I was arguing my case about pricing authority in front of a hundred salespeople. I expressed my conviction that salespeople should not have pricing authority for the reasons just stated. Everyone in the group, except for the president of the company, was satisfied and ready to move on.

He said to me, "But Tom, don't you think limited pricing authority makes sense?" As a speaker, it is never comfortable when the president of the company disagrees with you in front of the audience. I do not get to sign the back of the check until he signs the front. I knew the president of the company was a financial type and could answer my next question.

I asked, "What kind of range are we talking about?"

He said, "We don't give our salespeople full pricing authority. We give them a 20 percent range to work with."

My next question exposed the weakness in his logic. I asked, "What is the most common discount your salespeople give buyers?"

The color left his face, and he whispered, "Twenty percent." There was a collective gasp from the audience, and I looked at the president and said, "May we move on, please?" He nodded yes.

The moral of the story is, *if you give salespeople a 20 percent range, they will offer a 20 percent discount.*

In our longitudinal study of buyers and sellers, we asked 1,759 salespeople and their managers who would give their best customer a discount if the customer requested it. We found that 58 percent would give an average discount of 7.46 percent if the customer requested a lower price.

These examples are only a sample of the dozens of stories and statistics that I have accumulated over the years that support my argument about pricing authority. Should salespeople have this authority? From a psychological perspective, I could argue that they should, because it leads to job enrichment and greater ownership. From a marketing perspective, I must argue against pricing authority because too few salespeople (and some sales managers) approach it strategically. If there is a case to be made for when it is a good idea, I would like to hear it.

WHAT BUYERS REALLY WANT

If buyers want more than a cheap price, what is it? Since the early 1990s, I have studied this question extensively. We have conducted several studies of business-to-business buyers to identify their top priorities for each of the three dimensions of value: the product, the supplier of that product, and the salesperson. We provided a list of items for each dimension of value and asked the buyer to select the four most important items from each dimension. We then submitted their choices to a frequency distribution to compile a rank-ordering of their top preferences. Price ranked anywhere from nine in the early 1990s to six during the 2001 recession to eleven in our 2007 best sales practices (BSP) study. This means that even in the midst of an economic downturn, customers valued five things more than price. Our 2007 BSP research shows what buyers value most. The following illustrates buyer preferences for a solution in order of their importance to buyers.

Buyer Preferences Ranked by Importance
1. Product quality and performance
2. Customer service
3. Knowledgeable salespeople
4. Product availability
5. Supplier stands behind what he or she sells
6. Supplier is easy to do business with
7. Salesperson follows through on promises
8. Trustworthy salespeople
9. Product durability
10. Accessibility of salesperson
11. Product acquisition price
12. Technical support

When describing how salespeople bring value, fewer than 6 percent of our BSP respondents mentioned cheap price, and only 8 percent mentioned cost reductions. It may help to understand that our BSP respondents included more than four hundred end users or products, purchasing agents, and business owners. Buyers understand *that* value is more than a cheap price. Seventy-six percent said they would be willing to pay more for a better quality product, 67 percent would be willing to pay more for better service, and 68 percent said total cost of ownership was more important than acquisition price.

In a 2003 article, the use of price in the purchasing decision, the *Journal of Empirical Generalisations in Marketing Science* reported that 36 percent of shoppers never look for price information. That number climbs to 42 percent if the shopper is loyal to the store. Their research also indicated that only 19 percent switch because of price. This is about half the number that the retailers believed would switch for a cheaper price. Consider these numbers against the backdrop of consumer spending in discount stores. Wal-Mart has built a retailing fortress on the perception and expectation of everyday low prices. Could it be that the expectation is more relevant to the buying decision than the reality of lower prices? Many people claim Wal-Mart does not always have the cheapest prices on different items, but Wal-Mart owns that perception.

In an August 6, 2006, article in *Consumer Reports*, it was reported that car buyers rank price third behind fuel economy and reliability. The automotive industry is purportedly one of the most price-sensitive industries for sellers. A separate auto industry study, published in the April 2000 issue of *Consumer Reports*, found good treatment at the dealership ousted price as the most important consideration in choosing someplace to buy. Savvy car shoppers value something other than a cheap price. At the time of this writing, two of the Big Three U.S. automakers have filed for bankruptcy protection, notwithstanding their fear consumers will abandon manufacturers who seek bankruptcy protection. They sense something trumps a cheap price—fear. Buyers may be so fearful that a manufacturer will not be around to honor warranty claims that they will forgo a cheap price to deal with a manufacturer that is more financially stable. Fear generally trumps greed.

A 2006 National Shopping Behavior survey by KPMG found available inventory and ease of doing business eclipsed price for shopper preferences. Only 19 percent of buyers chose price as their determinant of where to buy.

The purpose for including all of these statistics is not to overwhelm you with numbers, although I can understand that reaction. Rather, it is to make the case that buyers want more than a cheap price. If price was the only factor that mattered, why would your company need salespeople? Follow the logic of this question. If price was all that mattered, companies would not need a sales force. All they would need is a price sheet, generated by the marketing department, sent out weekly to buyers: "Here is the cheapest price for our product this week. This is a link to our automatic order entry system. We have eliminated people totally. If you like our prices, buy from us." Why not just add, "If somebody else is cheaper, go with them."

If you really believe that price is all that matters, your profession, job, and future are on the endangered species list. Salespeople matter. Quality products matter. Follow-up service matters . . . to buyers. And that is ultimately what matters.

CHAPTER SUMMARY

Salespeople engage in self-deception when they believe price is all that matters. Most price objections are the result of self-inflicted wounds. Buyers want more than a cheap price. Quality, service, availability, and knowledgeable salespeople are attributes that they value over price. Challenging your belief that price is all that matters is a great first step in battling price resistance. Once you are convinced, you can turn to the task of convincing buyers that price is less important in the overall decision process.

5

Competing on Price

You cannot out-Wal-Mart Wal-Mart.

—ANONYMOUS

Unless your company is structured to operate as efficiently as Wal-Mart and enjoy their purchasing advantage, you cannot win a price battle against a company like this. Why choose to fight a price war on a battlefield your opponent already dominates? Many salespeople continue to attempt to compete this way when their companies are not equipped to support them.

This chapter explores

- the impact of competing on price alone and
- how and why salespeople delude themselves into believing that price battles are the only way to compete.

Once you have discovered the reality of profit destruction and market degeneration, you will understand why it is imperative that you hold the line on prices and retain your profitability.

THE CONSEQUENCES OF A PRICE-ONLY PHILOSOPHY

What would happen if you were to adopt a price-oriented, go-to-market strategy as your best-choice alternative? Here are the consequences. According to McKinsey & Company, a globally recognized leader in price consulting, slight declines in pricing can lead to huge decreases in profit. For example, the average S&P 1,000 company would suffer a 12.8 percent drop in profitability by giving a mere 1 percent discount, assuming no increase in volume. A 5 percent drop in price would require a 20 percent increase in volume to break even in operating profit.

If you earn a potential 40 percent gross margin and discount by 10 percent to save the sale, you must increase volume by 33 percent to maintain the same bottom-line profit. A 20 percent discount requires you to double your sales, and for a 30 percent discount, you must quadruple your sales—all to maintain the same net profit dollars.

Your marketing department works diligently to create an image for your company and your products. All of that can be negated by a renegade sales representative who cuts price to get an order. Multiply this by the entire sales force. If there are twelve salespeople in your company, you have twelve different product positions without price discipline. Discounting repositions your brand. When you cut price, you are saying, "Our product is not as good as the competition's product."

Discounting also affects the trust bond between you and buyers. Will they think you have been taking advantage of them all along? Once you begin discounting, buyers never feel secure in your prices. They always wonder if they got the best deal. This destroys the trust you have earned with them. How do you feel when you purchase something and discover you could have gotten a cheaper price?

When you cut price, you set a dangerous precedent. The law of gravity applies here. Once it goes down, it is not going up. Consider automobile sales. How many people pay sticker price for a new car? It does not happen often. Why? The precedent is set. The discounted price is the new reference point, and people talk. One thing price shoppers love to brag about is the great deal they got. Some exaggerate the deal, adding insult to injury.

In military parlance, you do not want to fight for the same ground twice. Once you begin discounting, you will fight for that ground again when it is time to raise prices. You owned that price before the discount. Now, you must fight again for that same piece of real estate. Plus, how much bigger will the price appear when you begin from a discounted price?

Once you adopt a price-only strategy, you start a price war. It signals to the competition your willingness to sell for less. If your competition is desperate, they will retaliate by cutting their prices, which means you must cut your prices again, and they, in turn, will need to continue the downward spiral. This scorched-earth madness continues until someone stops.

Salespeople who cut price earn less profit for their companies. Commissions drop, which means you personally earn less money. Your company has less money to invest in R&D and other product or service enhancements. Without that competitive advantage, you become more dependent on a price-only strategy. Following this death spiral to its natural conclusion is pricing yourself out of business.

Buyers want to feel that they are getting as good as they are giving. Sellers also have a need for equity in their transactions. One of the dark realities of a price-only strategy is when you give better than you get, you resent the business. Most salespeople can relate to taking a questionable piece of business and feeling resentful afterward because they gave more than they got. That is no way to build partnerships and long-term relationships with customers.

The old saying "Birds of a feather flock together" applies poignantly to price shoppers and price sellers, as they deserve each other. At a fundamental level, they understand each other's priorities and should do business with each other. Both want price to be as low as possible, and both will suffer the consequences of that approach.

Do you really want to tie up your resources in production and inventory management with price-sensitive accounts? When you stretch your resources thin to cover these high-volume, low-margin accounts, what is left for higher-margin buyers? If you have a volume/capacity focus, you have precious little time and resources for the niceties: relationship building, follow-up service, doing favors for the buyer, and the value-adds that you are accustomed to delivering. When you pursue volume and maximum capacity, you are so busy chasing deals that you will not have a chance to make a difference for the buyer.

When you compete on price only, you send the wrong message to the buyer. Indirectly, you are telling them, "Since price is all that matters, whenever somebody else with a cheaper price comes around, you should jump on that opportunity to buy cheaper." Essentially, you are inadvertently sending buyers to a cheaper competitor. You are acting as a proxy salesperson for your price-selling competitor.

When you adopt the attitude that the only way to compete is on price, you must make your money on the inside of your company. You contract and scale back—looking for ways to cut costs. You begin asking questions such as these:

- How can we cut costs?
- Can we cut a corner on quality?
- What if we downsize a couple of folks to become lean and mean?

You are relying on internal cost reductions to boost profitability because you are not making it on the outside. The ugly reality of price selling is that you are discounting the importance of your company's value-adds. Is this who you want to be? You cannot cut and contract your way to prosperity. You must expand, leverage, and sell your way to prosperity.

You can make money as a price seller if your company is structured that way. Most are not. Wal-Mart, Southwest Airlines, Home Depot, Best Buy, and other operationally efficient companies compete profitably at a lower price point because their business models support this marketing strategy. Unless your company has the buying power of Wal-Mart or the operational efficiency of Southwest Airlines, you will find it difficult to fight your marketing battle on the price battlefield. If you win a price war, it may be a Pyrrhic victory.

WHY SALESPEOPLE CUT PRICE

In light of all this information about the consequences of a price-only strategy, why do salespeople cut price? Here are seven common reasons why salespeople cut price.

1. Because they can. Companies give their salespeople authority to discount, oftentimes without adequate preparation and the information that they need to make prudent pricing decisions. Most salespeople lack the innate knowledge and skill to hold the line on pricing. Additionally, they may lack the discipline. The irony is shocking. What they lack they need to make prudent decisions. Instead of giving them training and policy guidelines, their companies give them authority to do what they are unprepared to do.

2. Lack of confidence or courage to hold the line in price negotiation. If you have never learned how to hold the line on pricing, you will discount. If you are not convinced that your solution is worth the price, you will discount. Courage, confidence, and resolve are powerful allies to accompany you in a negotiation.

3. Fear. Some salespeople fear losing the sale, losing a customer, or being perceived of as gouging the customer. Fear can be an inhibiting force. If you fear losing the business, is it because your product/solution's value is too low for the price that you are charging? Cutting price is only one way to respond to this. Adding value is an alternative to balance the value equation. Another benefit of adding value is that it assuages guilt because to effectively employ this negotiating strategy, you must understand the real value of your solution. Guilt comes from not understanding the full impact of your solution on the customer's business.

4. Mixed management signals. Managers may pay lip service to holding the line on pricing until volume drops or capacity idles. Then, they issue marching orders to the troops not to lose a sale because of price. If you are a manager reading this, do not confuse your salespeople by alternating your go-to-market strategies from a hold-the-line strategy to a discounting strategy. How can they have any confidence in your leadership when you change something as important as pricing policy? If you choose to compete on your total value, you must demonstrate the same courage you expect of your salespeople. This means you must maintain the integrity of your pricing discipline when things slow down.

5. Perception of weakness. Some salespeople are defensive about their price, because they feel powerless in the process. A purchasing agent once said to me, "Tom, if salespeople knew how powerful they really are, they would be dangerous. Any one of my suppliers has the power to shut down my production if they fail to perform. Yet their salespeople walk into my office, hat in hand, thinking that they are powerless in the negotiation."

6. Doubt. Some salespeople may doubt their personal value to the customer. They feel like they are part of the cost, not the value. These salespeople have no faith in themselves. They do not believe that they are personally worth the difference in price. They view themselves as a commodity. How can you feel good about charging more than the competition if you do not believe you personally deserve it?

7. Overidentification with customers. Some salespeople cut price because they overidentify with customers—a type of sales Stockholm syndrome. This syndrome was named after a 1973 Swedish bank robbery in Stockholm in which the robbers held bank employees for six days. The workers formed an emotional attachment to the robbers and later defended them in court. A Swedish psychiatrist observed this phenomenon and coined the term *Stockholm syndrome*.

When hostages identify with their captors, they are experiencing Stockholm syndrome. Salespeople can experience a similar phenomenon when their personal attachment to buyers clouds their vision and causes them to make decisions based on personal relationships rather than business principles. This is one reason you must maintain some professional distance so that you can make the tough decisions regarding your customers.

CHAPTER SUMMARY

The consequences of a price-oriented strategy can be disastrous. Unless your company is structured to compete as an operationally efficient organization, fighting the war on a price battlefield is ineffective and unprofitable. Competing on price damages your profit and your image. There are seven common reasons why salespeople cut price, and they often lack the will or skill to protect their price. To convince yourself of the dramatic impact of price reductions on your business, study the chain-of-event effects on your company of a price reduction. You will discover your attempt at short-term gain may result in long-term pain.

6

Price and Value

A cynic is someone who knows the price of everything and the value of nothing.

—OSCAR WILDE, IRISH PLAYWRIGHT, POET, AND AUTHOR

alue is the new euphemism for *cheap*. Advertisers tout *value pricing*. This confuses the marketplace and trivializes the concept of value. Everything on sale is not a value. It could be junk priced cheaply. The word *cheap* is not a politically incorrect word. It fully and accurately describes something of lower value. Price shoppers are not value shoppers. They both may want the best value for their money, but the price shopper's final decision rests on the money they exchange for the purchase. They want it cheap. Maybe we should call them *cheap shoppers.*

This chapter explains the critical difference between price and value. This distinction will help you understand the full impact of your solution on the customer. The key concepts in this chapter are

- the difference between price and value and
- the foundation for changing the way price shoppers think and buy.

At the end of this chapter, you will be able to focus your sales conversation on value, not just price.

VALUE IS MORE THAN A CHEAP PRICE

Value is an outcome. Unless you sell a precious commodity—such as metals or gems—or collectibles like art, the value of your product comes from what it *does*, not from what it *is*. The intrinsic value of most commercial products is negligible. Their worth comes from the value the products create for the buyer. Conversely, gold, silver, art, diamonds, and the like derive worth from their intrinsic value.

Value is also a personal thing. Like beauty, it is in the eye of the beholder. Each of us has a unique definition of value. Understanding the buyer's perspective helps you formulate a solution to maximize your value. This is the essence of customer-oriented selling—it is not value unless the customer says it is value.

Price is different from cost. Price is a short-term acquisition number that appears on an invoice. For example, if you sell a compressor for $375, the number 375 is *price* in our terminology. Cost is an inclusive, long-term number: usage cost, energy cost, replacement cost, repair cost, length of maintenance intervals, cost of ownership, training, installation, redistribution, and disposal cost. Cost extends throughout the life cycle of a product. Some people call this *total cost of ownership*.

Price is also different from value. Value is long-term. Price is what customers spend; value is what they receive. Value is the outcome of your product's benefits and the customer's experience with you and your company. Price is the buyer's input. When the outcome of a sale exceeds the buyer's input, the product/solution has great value. Value must be viewed as long-term impact. Price and cost are elements of value.

People from various disciplines have weighed in on the concept of value, and they share a common theme. John Ruskin wrote, "Value is the life-giving power of anything." What is the life-giving power of your solution? What is the outcome of your solution for the customer? Therein lies your value.

Management guru Peter Drucker wrote, "What the business thinks it produces is not of first importance . . . What the customer thinks he is buying, what he considers 'value,' is decisive . . . And what the customer buys and considers value is never a product. It is always *utility*, that is, what a product or service does for him." The *utility* of your solution is customer empowerment. What do you give the buyer the power to do?

Adam Smith wrote in *The Wealth of Nations*, "The real price of everything . . . is the toil and trouble of acquiring it." What you are willing to give up—

sacrifice—speaks loudly to what you value. The effort you are willing to make and the risk you are willing to take demonstrate what you value. If the buyer values your solution more than her funds, she will buy. Conversely, if she values her money more than your solution, she will object to your price.

Value involves a cost-benefit analysis by the buyer, "Is the product or service a fair exchange for what I give up in time, energy, and money to acquire it?" Is your solution equitable? As I have mentioned before, equity plays a major role in the buyer's perception of value: "Am I getting as good as I am giving?" At the heart of most price resistance is a perceived lack of equity. Buyers object to price when they feel they are giving more than they are getting.

Price shoppers are short-term thinkers. They lock in on acquisition price and lock out everything else, including the significant costs of owning, using, maintaining, and disposing of a solution you have not sold them yet.

Cost-based shoppers are savvier. They understand that the true cost of something extends beyond the acquisition point to the total cost of ownership. Their time horizon is longer than price shoppers' time horizon.

Value shoppers stand back further than cost shoppers and price shoppers to view the full scope of the solution on their business. They ask these questions:

- What does this solution enable us to do today that we could not do yesterday?
- What problems can we now solve that we have not been able to solve in the past?
- What new opportunities can we pursue now that we have not been able to pursue in the past?

These are value-oriented questions. The value shopper looks at the entire purchase as it affects him from cradle to grave. When the conversation fixates on price, you are discussing the short-term effect of your solution. Your immediate challenge is to change the conversation from price to cost to value, and in order to do this, you must understand the impact of your value on the buyer. Value is the outcome of the customer's investing in and implementing your solution. Which has a greater financial impact on the customer's bottom line—getting the cheapest price or the best value?

SELLING TO PRICE SHOPPERS

Selling profitably to price shoppers requires changing the way they view things—stretching their time horizons from short- to long-term and enlarging the conversation from price to money. These two fundamental concepts will drive your strategy throughout the remainder of this book.

Price shoppers have two vision problems that impair their judgment and decision making. First, they suffer from a kind of shortsightedness I call *price-shopper myopia*. This nearsighted approach to purchasing means they operate in the here and now and see only this moment, the acquisition point, and the acquisition price. This short-term view propels them to think *cheap*.

The second vision problem that afflicts price shoppers is tunnel vision. They fixate on the core-commodity naked product, ignoring the layers of value surrounding it. This means your value-added services, product enhancements, and personal support go largely unrecognized by tunnel-vision price shoppers.

To recap, the real problem with nearsighted, tunnel-vision price shoppers is that they focus narrowly on the now and the value-stripped product. The problem suggests the remedy: Help them see farther and broader. Stretch the time horizon and enlarge the discussion.

1. *Stretching the time horizon* **means encouraging the buyer to think, plan, and execute long-term versus short-term.** He must consider your long-term value, not just price. In Part II, I will give you more detailed guidance on how to do this with your questions and presentation, but here is a simple example of this concept at work. Ask the buyer this question: "Mr. Buyer, if you were to fast-forward a couple of years and look back on this decision, on what criteria would you judge its success?" Notice the buyer is forced to extend his outlook beyond the present to include the impact or outcome of this solution. This is the value of the solution—the long-term impact. If the seller is successful in getting the buyer to talk long-term, this is no longer a price discussion but a value discussion.

2. *Enlarging the discussion* **means expanding the buyer's peripheral vision from the core-commodity, naked product to your value-added solution.** As with the previous strategy, *stretching the time horizon*, this is covered fully later in the book. Here is an example of how you can enlarge the conversation with a simple question: "Mr. Buyer, you mentioned price as one of your concerns when you study the economic value of our solution. What else determines the financial success of this project?" The buyer has already mentioned price as a determinant. In this example, you are enlarging the discussion from price to money. Money is a better conversation than price to have with buyers because money is the larger issue—and can be affected by many factors.

Stretching and *enlarging* are the foundation of your strategy for selling profitably to price shoppers. Encouraging buyers to think long-term and consider the total impact of your solution is a better way for them to choose a solution, enabling them to take advantage of all the value in your proposition.

When you speak the language of the price shopper, you deprive him of the opportunity to capture the total value from your relationship and yourself the opportunity to stand out. Short-term, naked-product decisions ignore everything that makes you and your buyer's needs special. By accepting your product as a commodity, you are tacitly admitting there is nothing special about the buyer either. How do you think the buyer would react if you informed her she wasn't special? Who enjoys being told this?

CHAPTER SUMMARY

Value is different from cost or price. Price is a short-term decision variable. Cost is a longer-term consideration. Value is what a product is worth to the buyer either because of its intrinsic properties or because of what it does for the buyer in the long term. Price shoppers suffer from two vision problems. First, they are shortsighted, which means they concentrate on acquisition. Second, they suffer a form of tunnel vision, which means they lock in on the core-commodity, naked product. They ignore the layers of value that surround your product. Your strategy is to *stretch their time horizons* while expanding their mental peripheral vision by *enlarging the conversation*. As you do this, you change the discussion from price to value.

PART II

THE SHORTEST DISTANCE BETWEEN TWO POINTS IS A STRAIGHT LINE

This is true unless you are traveling the Büyük (Great) Menderes River in southwestern Turkey. Homer wrote about this in the *Iliad*. St. Paul traveled the area. This 363-mile river, the longest in the region, snakes a distance of about 155 miles as the crow flies from its headwaters in Afyon, Turkey, to its western destination, the Aegean Sea. The roots of the English word *meander* come from the Greek root, *Maiandros*, antiquity's name for this winding river.

A meandering river is the perfect metaphor for a disorganized sales presentation. When salespeople fail to gain early control of the sales conversation, the discussion can wander aimlessly to a nonconclusion or degenerate into a price-only decision. Gaining a preemptive selling advantage means establishing early, positive control and guiding the conversational flow down a stream of value, not price.

By reading Part II and applying these ideas, you will control the conversational flow and gain a preemptive selling advantage by stretching the buyer's time horizon and enlarging the conversation beyond the core-commodity, naked-product discussion of the price shopper.

7

Preparing to Sell in a Price-Sensitive Market

No one plans to fail, but many fail to plan.

—ANONYMOUS

I do not know who originally said this, but I have a pretty good idea how many sales managers and trainers have echoed this over the years. There are several legitimate reasons to lose a sale—lack of availability, wrong product for an application, lack of funding for an idea, or soft demand. Lack of preparation is not a legitimate reason to lose a sale. I have mentioned this before, but it bears repeating that you never want to go to a negotiation being out-prepared by the buyer for the negotiation, especially if you know it involves a tug-of-war over price.

This chapter is about planning and preparation. There is a formula that I have used in my own business for years: P + P = 2P. Planning and preparation equal twice the performance. Three kinds of preparation are discussed in this chapter:

- Personal preparation
- Collateral preparation
- Call preparation

At the end of this chapter, you will be able to level the playing field by preparing thoroughly for your sales calls and price negotiations.

THE IMPORTANCE OF BEING PROACTIVE

Positive anticipation is the logical outcome of a positive attitude. Being proactive means thinking now about later—creating the future in the now. It is developing the rock-deep roots of mental preparation to steady you when the winds of resistance start to blow. It is about being prepared for the unknown. It is planned spontaneity.

Avoiding price objections is your best strategy. Dealing proactively with price objections allows you to shift the focus off price by presenting a compelling argument before the buyer raises the objection and taking ownership of the price question so the buyer feels no need to raise it or defend it.

Planning and preparation build confidence and proficiency. When your confidence increases, your competence increases. A common denominator among professionals is that they prepare. Airline pilots conduct a lengthy preflight routine to ensure safety. They study weather conditions and plan their travel route accordingly. Their checklist includes walking around the airplane, checking the instruments, and testing equipment. Doctors prepare meticulously before surgery. CPAs prepare extensively for IRS audits. Are salespeople any less professional than these folks? Only if they fail to plan. A Dartnell study of 1,670 sales managers and top salespeople discovered that when asked to rank order the most critical skills for their long-term success, they ranked planning first.

PERSONAL PREPARATION

Be a serious student of your profession. Invest in your own personal research and development to build your knowledge base by studying the sales process and understanding your product.

Since 1990, buyers have told us in our surveys that the number one quality they look for in salespeople is knowledge. They want to deal with experts. Becoming an expert in your field sets you apart from the competition. It is a personal positioning strategy that brands you as the best.

Sir Francis Bacon wrote, "Knowledge is power." Thomas Edison wrote, "The value of an idea lies in the using of it." Knowledge is like kindness, love, and hope. They all increase in value as you share them with others. Sharing knowledge with buyers is a compelling response to the question, Why should I do business with you?

If you were an auto mechanic, you would own at least forty thousand dollars worth of tools. It is part of the job—an investment in your career. Similarly, salespeople must make significant investments in themselves. Invest in your intellectual capital. Study to increase your expertise, and invest in the best tools you can find to enhance the quality of your work.

At a national sales meeting, I presented an award to a sales rep who distinguished himself among his peers. The managers referred to him as a "three percenter." I asked, "What is a 'three percenter'?" They answered that every year this sales rep invested 3 percent of his own time and money into his own professional development. He believed if he invested 3 percent of his time and money into his own professional development, he would be in the top 3 percent of all salespeople in his profession. He was number one in a sales force of five hundred!

What significant investments have you made in yourself recently? What is in your professional library? How have you invested in the tools to help you become a better sales rep? How often do you attend training sessions to boost your knowledge? How often do you read books or news pertaining to the sales profession? Investing in your knowledge is a critical part of your strategy for avoiding price objections. Refer to the sidebar "Build Your Knowledge Base" for a list of questions that are helpful to ask yourself.

Warfighting, a book on military strategy written by the U.S. Marine Corps staff, discusses the importance of preparation before going into battle. An army at war spends time fighting, but an army during peacetime spends a great deal of time preparing for the next battle. Preparation is a critical success factor for any military operation. This book explains how several battles were turned because of opportunity. The military force that was better prepared to deal with an opportunity when it surfaced during battle won because they were ready, willing, and able to seize the moment. This reminds me of the old saying, Luck is where preparation meets opportunity.

This is especially relevant for salespeople. You prepare by arming yourself with knowledge about your company and your buyer. Combined with competitive intelligence, preparation gives you an arsenal of information to capitalize on selling opportunities you encounter.

Knowing a competitor's weakness is not negative selling. It is just competition, and your competitor would not hesitate to capitalize on a competitive advantage over you. This is why it is vital to have competitive knowledge. Know your product well. Understand your value added from the inside out. Develop an in-depth understanding of your buyer's needs. Be prepared to seize the opportunity to take advantage of a competitor's vulnerability.

Build Your Knowledge Base

This list of questions about your company, your competition, and your buyer will help you build your knowledge base:

- What is our mission?
- What business are we in?
- Where is our company headed?
- What values does our company stand for?
- Are we known for our innovative products, how we serve buyers, or the efficiencies in our operations?
- How are we positioned in the industry?
- What are our core competencies or specialized expertise?
- How are we strong?
- How are we vulnerable?
- Who are our primary competitors?
- Where are they strong?
- How are they vulnerable?
- How do we compare to the competition along these three dimensions of value: our products, our people, and our company?
- Who are our ideal customers?
- What do our best customers look for in a solution? (i.e., a product, a company, or its people)
- When we are successful with customers, why?
- Why will our customers pay more to do business with us?
- What factors eat away at our customer's profitability?
- What would our customers like to be able to do tomorrow that they cannot do today?

COLLATERAL PREPARATION

To be able to stretch the buyer's time horizon and shift the conversation from price to cost to value, you must understand the impact of your value on the buyer. To develop this insight, it is useful to create selling tools to use in your customer messaging campaign. *Customer messaging* is the ongoing conversation with customers about your value. In this case, your messaging strategy is to surround the buyer with your value story to take the focus off price. In this section, you will learn how to create several customer messaging tools and suggestions for their use.

VIP List

The first tool is the value-in-purchasing (VIP) list. It is a list of all the value added your company delivers along the three dimensions of value: product value, company value, and salesperson value. The VIP list reads like a smorgasbord of value for your buyer. It can be a fancy brochure or a simple list on your company letterhead. One way to enhance the VIP list is to attach a dollar value to the impact of these items on the buyers—what it is worth to them. One additional benefit to you as a salesperson of creating the VIP list is that it acts as a centering exercise as it reminds you of the reasons why your solution (product, company, and you) is special.

Use the VIP list as a positioning tool to enhance your image and educate the buyer. Include it as a page in a proposal. Present it to the buyer as a promise on the front end of the sale and as a performance appraisal tool to document your value once the solution is in place. Make it a page on your website. Use it to deal with price objections. When the buyer rejects your price, you can respond, "I understand your concern about money. My concern is what we must remove from our list of value to meet the price you are willing to pay. I don't think either of us wants that."

The only thing that limits your use of this tool is the edge of your imagination. Do not wait for your company to create this for you. You are losing valuable time. Grab your company letterhead and create it. If your company prepares something more formal and professional, that is a bonus!

Value Proposition

The second tool is the *value proposition*. A value proposition is simply the outcome of your customer's experience—the result of the customer's benefit from all of the value added on your VIP list. The value proposition answers these types of questions:

- How do you help your customers compete better in their market?
- How do you help them increase their customers' satisfaction?
- How do you help your customers do a better job at whatever they do?

Understanding your value proposition is an important part of convincing buyers that they should consider everything you do, not just the price you offer. Communicating your value proposition is essential to stretching the buyer's time horizon, since your focus is on outcome. When you concentrate on results, acquisition price is less important.

The value proposition appeals to a specific group of customers with common needs called a *segment*. When segmenting customers, assign them by the complexity or simplicity of their needs. Buyers with complex needs are more open to value-added solutions. Buyers with simple needs are more price sensitive. The tighter your definition of customer segments, the more compelling your value proposition.

Next, identify how you bring value to them. Think long-term outcome or down-line impact of your customer experience. Your value proposition is the result of the customer's experience with your value added. Build it by completing this statement: "When customers employ our solution, they can anticipate this outcome." For example, if you sell to small electrical contractors, study the common needs of small electrical contractors. They may need to deal with a supplier who carries vast inventory and can ship orders quickly. Your value proposition to them might be quick turnaround of orders with a high fill rate, both of which enable them to compete more aggressively in their market.

The value proposition is like an executive summary of the impact of your solution. It is what you do for the buyer. Because it succinctly encapsulates your impact, you can use it as a powerful overview statement for customers. The rest of your presentation will focus in-depth on how you will bring this value to the customer. Think of using the value proposition as a way to preview your solution and its impact. The VIP list is a detailed version of how you deliver your value proposition.

Unique Selling Proposition

This third tool is the one thing you can lay claim to that nobody else in the industry can say. It is the answer to the question "What are your definable and defendable differences?"

Most salespeople fail to differentiate themselves from the competition. Three separate studies demonstrate that this is a major cause of price objections. Buyers do not perceive a dime's worth of difference between one solution and another. Why should they pay more for the higher-priced solution? Knowing your unique selling proposition (USP) and integrating it into your sales conversation adds critical degrees of separation between you and the competition, making it easier for you and the buyer to justify the difference in pricing.

When constructing your USP, keep it short and specific—fifty words or less. Pick something visible and valuable to the customer, and it must be a defendable position by your company.

By completing the following statements, you will identify your USP:

- ■ We are the only ones in the marketplace that . . .
- ■ We were the first ones in the industry to . . .
- ■ Customers tell us we really stand out because of . . .

How you finish those statements is your USP. For buyers to pay a higher price from you versus the competition, they must understand and appreciate the differences between you and the competition.

"Ten Things to Consider" List

List ten areas for which you enjoy competitive advantages. Turn them into selling points, in the form of a "ten things to consider when buying" list for your buyer.

These questions will help you build this list:

- ■ What is unique about your products?
- ■ What is unique about your company?
- ■ What is unique about you as a salesperson?

One of my customers turned these competitive differences into a brochure. He called it *Ten Questions to Ask Before Making a Major Purchase*. Each question highlights a unique strength that he brings to the table. These strengths are his competitors' weaknesses. On one hand, he discusses his value added. On the other hand, he subtly calls attention to a competitor's weakness without bad-mouthing. This is seizing opportunity in the heat of battle.

The "ten things to consider" list makes it easer for the buyer to justify the difference in your pricing. With ten points of differentiation, your price will naturally be higher. You can use this list in your presentation as part of your differentiating strategy. It can be a page in a proposal. You may fax or e-mail this list to a buyer if she is sitting on the fence and need a nudge to move in your direction.

Testimonials Sheet

Our final tool reassures buyers that others enjoy success with your solution. Having other well-respected people endorse something is comforting and builds credibility. During periods of uncertainty, people gravitate toward the pack.

The testimonials sheet is a one-page document titled, for instance, "What Others Are Saying." It provides for your customers several testimonial quotes from opinion leaders in a target industry. It works for a couple of reasons. One, seeing these quotes on one page has great visual impact on the buyer. Two, it is easier to get short endorsements versus an entire letter. Call the customer and ask, "Would you do me a favor? Please write a couple of sentences about your experience with our company and e-mail it to me. I'm assembling a testimonials page for a proposal." Make it easy for the customer to help you.

Once you complete your testimonial page, e-mail a copy to the endorser to demonstrate your work. There is a benefit to this customer seeing her opinion aligned with other industry leaders. Use the testimonials sheet in proposals and during presentations when you feel the buyer needs reassurance. A good way to present it is, "Would you like to read what others have said about our solution?" Then, hand over the testimonial sheet to the buyer.

CALL PREPARATION

In our best practices research, we discovered 95 percent of top-achieving sales-people prepare for sales calls. When preparing for a sales call involving price discussions, you must be ready. Again, you do not want to be out-prepared by the buyer for this meeting. These four questions will help you ready yourself for this meeting:

- What do I want to accomplish on this call?
- Why will price be an issue, and how do I know this?
- How will I stretch the buyer's time horizon and enlarge the discussion beyond price?
- What will I ask the buyer to do at the end of the meeting?

When I share this list of questions with salespeople in seminars, I ask what they think would happen if they asked themselves these questions before every sales call. They respond that they would be better prepared and more effective as a result.

Planning is like not planning in that both become habitual with time. You may want to take this a step further and create a "call planning guide" to lay out your strategy on paper. Top-achieving salespeople do what others consider to be a hassle.

CHAPTER SUMMARY

Professionals prepare and rehearse before they perform. You see this in all walks of life. In professional sports, teams prepare for each game. They study their opponents' strengths and weaknesses and build a game plan to maximize their own performance. It is difficult to imagine sustainable success without preparation. Isolated examples exist as dumb luck, but that is no foundation upon which to build your long-term success. Professional salespeople prepare themselves for their meetings with buyers. They do not want to be out-prepared by the buyer for the price negotiation. Salespeople prepare by building their knowledge base, preparing collateral support tools, and planning their sales calls. Make planning a discipline, and you will be prepared for the toughest selling situations.

8

Preemptive Probing

There is a great difference between knowing and understanding: You can know a lot about something and not really understand it.
—CHARLES F. KETTERING, INVENTOR AND FORMER HEAD OF
GENERAL MOTORS RESEARCH

Charles Kettering was an American inventor with more than three hundred patents, founder of Delco, and head of General Motors research for twenty-seven years. He knew about understanding. Salespeople often think they know their buyer's needs. Buyers often think they know their own needs. Does either really understand the depth and complexity of the buyer's needs?

This chapter is about understanding. For you, as a salesperson, it is about developing an in-depth understanding of the buyer's needs. For the buyer, it is about developing a comprehensive understanding of his or her own needs. Price shoppers focus on short-term, commodity-acquisition needs. Your challenge is to help them understand the full scope of their needs. This greater understanding paves the way for the buyer's openness and acceptance of the value from your solution. This chapter explores these facets of buyer decision making:

- Buyer motivation and the forces that influence their decisions
- The difference between needs and wants

■ How fear affects buying decisions
■ How to use questions to shift the buyer's focus off price

At the end of this chapter, you will be able to understand fully the buyer's needs and help the buyer develop this same understanding of their needs.

THE DYNAMICS OF BUYING AND SELLING

What causes a buyer to pay more for your product? What is more compelling than a cheaper price? What is the full scope of the buyer's needs? The most effective way to answer these questions is to ask them and listen to the buyer. Buying and selling is an information exchange. The buyer gives you information, and you in turn input that information, process it, and output a solution. Ideally, the solution you output overlaps the buyer's needs. The greater the overlap between your solution and the buyer's needs, the greater the probability you will make the sale. Your goal is to achieve maximum overlap. Preemptive probing helps you with the first half of this process—gaining information.

UNDERSTANDING BUYER MOTIVATION

Purchasing involves reason and emotion. Blaise Pascal said, "The heart has reasons which reason doesn't understand." Understanding a buyer's motivation helps you become a better salesperson and provide a better solution. Buyers' needs are often more complex than price shoppers admit. Here is what we know about buyer motivation:

■ **Buyers do things for their own reasons, not yours.** They do not care about your reasons for selling. They are totally focused on their situation. The prevailing question in the buyer's mind is, "What's in it for me?" A buyer's concern for a supplier grows from a deeper concern for her own welfare.

■ **Everyone is concerned about something other than price.** Even the most price-sensitive individual has something that bothers him more than paying too much for something.

■ **Emotion is a more powerful motivator than reason.** People tend to make emotional decisions and use reason to justify the decision. If humans made purely rational decisions, they would not smoke, abuse alcohol, or eat excessively. As you ask questions and listen to the buyer's responses, you gain insight into the emotions that drive his decisions.

■ **The newest research on buying behavior estimates that as many as 90 percent of buying decisions could be made on the subconscious level.** Buyers are oblivious to all the reasons they act. This is why positioning plays an important role in persuading buyers. Your customer-messaging campaign predisposes the buyer to your solution. It prepares the battlefield of the buyer's mind for the discussion of value.

■ **Buyers feel both satisfaction and dissatisfaction simultaneously with products.** There are qualities they like and qualities they dislike about what they buy. Dissatisfaction drives change. People change when the pain is greater than the gain. The greater the dissatisfaction, the greater their motivation is to change. Pain avoidance is often a more powerful motivator than pursuit of gain. Pain and fear are the most misunderstood and maligned human emotions. They can be friend or foe depending on how you use them in the sale.

■ **Equity motivates people to act.** Everyone wants to feel that she is treated fairly in a transaction—that she gets as good as she gives. The important thing to remember about equity is how it exists in the buyer's mind. It is important that you feel equity; it is imperative the buyer feels equity.

NEEDS, WANTS, AND FEARS

Do you really know what buyers *need* in a solution? Do you know what they *want*? Do you know what they *fear*? There are outcomes buyers hope to achieve and those they hope to avoid. Buyers desire more gains: profit, productivity, performance, convenience, quality, and safety. They desire less pains: hassles, back orders, waiting time, breakdowns, mistakes, downtime, and problems. Helping your buyer satisfy both priorities increases your probability of success.

In Chapter 2, we defined needs as something that *must* happen and wants as something that buyers would *like* to see happen. In this chapter, we expand the definition of needs and wants. *Needs* are reason-based, objective buying criteria. For example, a buyer needs transportation, quality standards, compliance to specifications, delivery, and product availability. Buying criteria answer the questions, "What do you need in a product?" "What do you require in a solution?" or "What are your expectations from a supplier?" Needs have an organizational focus.

Wants are emotion-based, subjective desires. These are niceties versus necessities. They satisfy a personal win. Someone *needs* transportation but may *want* style, image, or economy. Wants focus on personal issues like achieving consensus among all the people involved in a buying decision, increased control, no surprises, something easy to operate and maintain, safety, appreciation for a job well-done, or recognition. It is the buyer's answer to your question, "What do you personally want to achieve with this purchase?"

Fears represent situations buyers want to avoid when purchasing. Fears keep them awake at night and are chock-full of emotion. People want to avoid mistakes like the call at 2 A.M., asking, "Where is our stuff?" Other mistakes include peer resistance to an idea, too much exposure, too much to do, and paying too much for something. It is the answer to this question: "What concerns you most when making this buying decision?"

Discovering what buyers need, want, and fear increases effectiveness. One study found salespeople who sell to the buyer's needs and wants are more likely to close the sale at a higher gross margin. Another study demonstrated two-thirds of self-acknowledged price-shopping purchasing agents admitted to legally changing the specifications on a quotation to reflect the solution from a salesperson who understood their needs and wants. This demonstrates the power of emotion in buying decisions. Humans are emotional creatures who often use reason to justify their emotional decisions to act. Price shoppers admit that your understanding of their personal wins increases your probability of success. There is an old saying in sales: sell 'em what they want and give 'em what they need.

PREEMPTIVE PROBING

This is the single best investment of your selling time. There are a number of advantages of probing:

- It puts the spotlight where it belongs—on the buyer, not you. It is his money and their problem. The sale should be more about the customer.
- Probing gives you critical information you need to prescribe the right solution and shift the focus off price.
- Probing involves the buyer. Psychological studies demonstrate that involvement lowers resistance to change. The more people are engaged

in the change process, the more ownership they feel. This buy-in generates greater support for your solution as it becomes their solution.

■ Probing and directing attention to non-price issues demonstrates your competence by spotlighting other critical areas. Buyers will then realize that you understand everything that is important in the buying decision.

■ When you listen actively to the buyer's needs, you exhibit a genuine concern to make his life better. This earns the buyer's trust, and people like to do business with those whom they trust.

A fundamental value-added selling principle is that buyers who understand the complexity of their needs are more open to value-added solutions. In this case, buyers who understand that their needs transcend price are willing to pay more for a better solution.

SHIFTING THE BUYER'S FOCUS

Gaining a preemptive selling advantage is a three-part strategy. The first part, as discussed in the previous chapter, is preparation. The next step is shifting the buyer's focus, changing the buyer's thinking by stretching the time horizon and enlarging the discussion. Help the buyer make bigger and better decisions than price decisions. This begins by his understanding of the full scope of his needs. To help the buyer understand fully his needs, study these questions:

■ How would the buyer choose if he did not need to concentrate on price?
■ What is the best possible decision the buyer could make?
■ What is the best way for the buyer to solve this problem?
■ What is the ideal outcome for the buyer?
■ What does long-term success look like to this buyer?

Each of these questions seeks to eliminate price as the single decision criterion.

Help the buyer simplify the decision process. You want the buyer to develop a deeper and broader understanding of his needs. Go beyond basic or generic needs. Drill down on the buyer's definition of value. Help him to think, plan, and execute better. Your strategy for doing this is *preemptive probing*.

Buyers must understand the impact of their buying decision—the consequences of moving forward and the impact of inertia. The impact of inertia refers to the opportunity cost of failing to act—what it costs the buyer to miss an opportunity. This is outcome-oriented selling. Shifting the buyer's focus to outcome initiates a conversation about the long-term consequences of his or her decisions. Outcome is a value conversation. The outcome of the buyer's employing your value-added solution is your value proposition. As he visualizes a successful outcome, the buyer's mind is opened to a more complete solution.

Outcome describes the results of a decision. Acquisition price is an input variable in the purchasing decision. Value is an outcome. Buyers live longer— for better or worse—with the outcomes of the decision than they do with input variables like price. Price is long forgotten after the solution is in place. Can you remember the price you paid for your last television or major appliance?

Understanding the buyer's perspective empowers you to sell value, not price. It helps you develop integrity in your pricing program because you understand the financial impact of your solution on the customer. Your pricing becomes value-based.

Research demonstrates that your understanding the quantitative value of your benefits to the customer helps you to capture more value from your market. What is your solution worth to the buyers? What impact does your value have on their lives? This information comes from asking the right questions. The following list of questions will help you shift the buyer's focus.

Ask Questions to Stretch Your Buyer's Time Horizon

Call attention to long-term value issues, not just short-term price issues. If you stretch the time horizon, you have an opportunity to discuss the extra services you offer. Here are some examples:

- How long do you plan to own or use this product?
- When you reflect on this decision two years down the road, on what criteria will you judge the effectiveness of the solution?
- What are your long-term goals for this project?
- Where would you like to go in the future with this?
- What long-term requirements do you have?
- Where do you see your company headed in the future?
- Walk me through your project start to finish.
- How do you determine total cost of ownership?
- How do you conduct a value analysis?
- What does a successful outcome look like to you?
- Are you looking for a short-term fix or long-term solution?

Ask Questions That Call Attention to Broad-Based, Non-Price Issues

Buyers who understand the complexity of their needs are more open to non-price solutions. Consider incorporating any of the following questions into a relevant discussion:

- What are the most important trends in your industry?
- What do your buyers look for from you?
- What are some drains on your profitability?
- What special delivery requirements do you have?
- Do you have any special packaging issues?
- How much technical support do you require?
- How do you define value?
- What do you want to gain with this solution?

Ask Questions That Call Attention to Your Value Added

This begins with your knowledge of your value-added extras. By asking these kinds of questions, you suggest these are strengths for your company and encourage the buyer to consider issues beyond price:

- How much flexibility do you need from a supplier?
- What can we do to make it easier for you to buy from us?
- What quality issues concern you the most?
- What special ordering needs do you have?
- Is electronic commerce important to you?
- Do you need help training your employees?
- Is it important for your suppliers to offer this type of service?

Ask Questions That Spotlight a Competitor's Weakness

Avoid negative selling or bad-mouthing the competition. Create an awareness of any weaknesses, and give the buyer an opportunity to elaborate. Focus on those areas where you know your competitor is vulnerable and you happen to be strong, for example:

- How is the quality of what you are using now?
- What do you like or dislike about what you currently use?
- Will the product you are currently using get you where you want to be in the future?

- What kind of feedback do you get from your folks on what you are currently using?
- How is the delivery?
- What experiences have you had with this product?

Observe this caveat: you must earn the right to ask competitive questions. Do not open with these questions. Lead with long-term, non-price, needs-oriented questions, and work your way into competitive questions. Use conversation starters buyers prefer to answer. Then, you may ask these questions.

Ask Questions to Create a Positive Sense of Urgency

Why should the buyer act on her decision? A positive sense of urgency can be a powerful motivator. It reinforces the buyer's need to act now. The following questions can highlight how time should displace price in a buying decision:

- How quickly do you want to move on this?
- What does a delay cost your company?
- What are your short-term goals?
- What advantage is there in waiting?
- In what ways are you not getting full utilization from your current solution, and how does that affect your company?

Your purpose is to support the buyer's need to move on something. Buyers procrastinate and avoid making decisions. A body at rest tends to remain at rest. A body in motion tends to remain in motion. Positively nudge the buyer.

Tap Into Your Buyer's Hope for the Future

Encourage the buyer to dream the impossible dream. Hope is a powerful motivator. Focusing the buyer's attention on the hope and optimism of a successful outcome can overshadow the concern for a cheaper price. Here are some questions that might spark this hope in your buyer:

- What do you want to see happen as a result of your company moving forward on this project?
- Once this solution is in place, what will success look like to you?
- What would you like us to do for you that no one else can?
- If you were to create the ideal solution, what would it look like?
- If you had unlimited funding for this project, what would you do? Why?

- If you were a supplier, what would you offer buyers like yourself that no one else offers?
- If you could change just one thing, what would it be? How would that help your business?

These questions expose the gap between what he currently uses and where he would like to be.

Ask Questions to Elicit Buyer Concerns or Fears

There are outcomes that the buyer wants to achieve and those he wants to avoid in a purchase. Oftentimes, avoiding pain is a more powerful motivator than pursuing gain. Fear trumps most other emotions, including greed. If you can expose these concerns, you can prescribe the right solution to alleviate their fears. Here are some example questions to ask:

- What concerns you most about making this buying decision?
- What is your greatest fear with this purchase?
- What do you want to avoid in moving forward?
- What would inhibit your moving forward?
- Do you see any reason you would not go forward and purchase this solution?
- What do you dislike doing that we can do for you?

With these questions, you tap into the buyer's fears so you can relieve these with your solution.

Get to Price Indirectly

Understanding the buyer's price sensitivity can help you determine how challenging it will be to make your case. It is difficult to ask directly about price without biasing the buyer's response. Avoid this by asking indirect questions:

- Tell me about your decision process. (A good reply from the buyer enables you to determine if she is going to bid a particular piece of business or if price is an issue.)
- What factors go into your buying decision?
- What are you looking for in a product?
- What are the three most important things you want in a solution?

If you must ask a question about budget, ask, "What budget range are you working with?" The word *range* implies flexibility. Listen to the range the buyer gives you, and use the higher number if price becomes an issue. Here is another way to frame this question: "What is your target range for cost on this project?" The word *target* also implies flexibility.

These lists of questions will change your selling life forever. Copy them. Carry them with you. Use them proactively to take the spotlight off price and to gain a preemptive selling advantage.

CHAPTER SUMMARY

Now you have the second part of your three-part strategy to achieve a preemptive selling advantage by using questions. Buying and selling is an information exchange. Questions facilitate this exchange. Buyers have needs, wants, and fears. Buyers who are aware of the complexity of their needs are more open to value-added solutions. Questions are magical. You can change the buyer's mind in your favor by asking the right questions. Asking questions that help buyers focus on long-term, non-price issues pave the way for you to discuss your value-added solution. Buyers who recognize these needs will hear your message loud and clear. Your challenge is to understand fully your buyer's needs. The questions in this chapter will change your selling life forever.

9

Presenting Your Solution

Fairy tales are more than true: not because they tell us that dragons
exist, but because they tell us that dragons can be beaten.
—G. K. CHESTERTON, TWENTIETH-CENTURY ENGLISH WRITER

To repeat a theme from earlier in this book: you can slay the price dragon. Your presentation is not a fairy tale, but a tale of the fair exchange of resources for a solution of value. You have a compelling reason for why the buyer should choose your alternative; all you need is a model for presenting this. In the previous chapter, you learned that buying and selling is an information exchange. Your questions have opened the buyer's mind and eyes to the depth and breadth of his or her needs. Now it is time to present your argument.

To review, achieving your preemptive selling advantage is a three-part strategy. The first part of this strategy is personal, collateral, and call preparation. Preemptive probing is the second part. This chapter is about the third and final part of your strategy for gaining a preemptive selling advantage, changing the conversation. You can change the conversation and the buyer's mind with your story of value. These key concepts discussed in this chapter will help you construct and tell your value story:

- What it means to change the conversation with the buyer
- Nine ways to enhance your presentation
- How to present your price to the buyer

At the end of this chapter, you will be able to present a compelling and enthusiastic argument for why your solution is a fair exchange for the buyer's energy and resources to acquire it.

CHANGE THE CONVERSATION

Once you have enlarged the definition of the buyer's needs via preparation and probing, you can enlarge the definition of your solution. Your focus is on a total value-added solution, not just the core-commodity, naked-product fix that price shoppers want. This expanded discussion means you get to tell a more complete story.

Changing the conversation means stretching the buyer's time horizon and discussing the advantages of a partnership with your company versus the short-term gain of a cheap price. This is the difference between a value-added, long-term solution and a quick-fix approach to problem solving. You can change the conversation to sell conceptually the importance of purchasing a value-added solution by focusing on the results that come from your solution. The goal is to change the buyer's focus from an obsession on input variables like price to understanding and appreciating the value in the results. Changing the conversation is moving away from adversarial negotiating positions that dominate price discussions to a more cooperative, value-added partnership—a loyal relationship between buyer and seller. This redefining of your relationship is the cornerstone of future business.

PRESENTATION ENHANCEMENT

Changing the conversation from price to value means changing the way you present your solution to the buyer. These nine presentation-enhancement ideas are designed to help you rethink the content and context of your argument.

1. Use Analogies

Analogies inject dynamite into your presentation and allow for the comparison of a familiar idea with an unfamiliar one. In sales, the analogy is powerful because you can identify another area in the buyer's business where he has made a similar buying decision and then draw an analogy between your product and the other item. Adults tend to act on precedent. If you demonstrate to a buyer that he has made non-price decisions in other areas, he will be more open to your idea.

A safety products sales manager told me about his experience with using analogies. One of his products is a safety harness for workers on scaffolds. He got a price objection because his safety harness was priced higher than the competition's.

The buyer said, "I think I should just go with the cheaper product."

The sales manager knew the buyer had just purchased a new truck, so he asked, "If you were to suspend your new truck from a scaffold using either of these two harnesses, which would you choose?"

The buyer responded, "Yours, of course. It's a better harness."

The sales manager responded, "Wouldn't you want the same safety for your workers that you want for a truck?" The buyer conceded the point, and the sales manager made the sale.

My files are filled with examples of analogies salespeople have used over the years to seal the deal: "You are willing to make a value-added decision in other areas. Doesn't it make sense to do that in this case as well?"

Once I was making joint calls with a salesperson for a well-known brewery. We called on a restaurant that had just invested several hundred thousand dollars upgrading its image to appeal to an upscale audience: menu, fixtures, and furniture. The only problem was that their draught product did not reflect the image they created in all these other areas.

This was an easy sale for the beer salesperson. She pointed out to the buyer that he had invested heavily in all those areas and it made sense to have a draught product that reflected the image he wanted to project. That analogy proved to be a powerful motivator for the buyer. It is no surprise the premium beer they ended up putting on draught was the more expensive alternative the sales rep sold.

Look for relevant analogies in the buyer's world that help make your case. One creative salesperson used the buyer's own literature to make his argument. He selected passages from the buyer's annual report that demonstrated their commitment to excellence, quality, and top-of-the-line products. He wove these into his presentation by saying, "In studying your annual report, many of the ways you describe your product remind me of what we sell. Two companies that think this much alike should do business, don't you think?" He presented a compelling argument by using the analogy of the buyer's advertising message. This made it easier for the buyer to pay more. It was difficult for the buyer to argue against his own advertising message and go-to-market strategy.

2. Give the Buyer Permission to Pay More for Your Product

Sometimes, buyers need a nudge to spend more than they anticipated. This is similar to the common advertising theme "When you deserve the best." It sounds like this: "Mr. Buyer, you have invested heavily in every other area in this project to ensure you get everything you need to do the job you want to do. Wouldn't it make more sense to go ahead and pay a little more than you anticipated for this item than to regret it on the back end?" Give the buyer permission to invest in your solution. Convince her that she has earned the right to use the best. There are buyers who need to be reassured that it is OK to spend a little more than they anticipated.

You can use an analogy to boost your argument. Illustrating how the buyer has spent more in other critical areas can be a compelling argument: "It is OK to apply that same purchasing logic to this situation, also. You deserve the best from us to go with the other smart buying decisions you've made."

3. Position Your Solution as an Investment, Not an Expense

Buyers view your product or service as either an expense or an investment. If they view it as an expense, they see it as a necessary cost of doing business, and most likely, price dominates the decision. If they view it as an investment, they are more focused on the money returning to their company—the return on their investment—than the money leaving their company.

When you position your solution as an investment, you may present it as an investment in their product quality, their customers' satisfaction, or their competitive advantage. Ask yourself this question: "How does my solution represent an investment, not an expense, to my customer?" The return on that investment is the crux of your argument. Remember, the fundamental strategy for dealing with any price objection is to keep the focus long-term. Selling the investment value of your products is a long-term sale.

4. Acknowledge the Immediate Impact of Price While Focusing on the Down-Line Benefit of Ownership

Customers buy results. When you stress results—what buyers can expect as a consequence of working with you—and maintain the focus on down-line, back-end value added, you mitigate the short-term impact of price in the decision process. Keep your focus long-term.

The buying decision includes input variables or decision criteria like price, availability, delivery, packaging, etc. The common denominator is that these are short-term considerations, immediate-impact issues. The decision to do something different is driven by a desire for a long-term outcome. Outcome is at the other end of the time continuum. It includes things like efficiency, quality, competitive gain, and increased market share.

You can acknowledge the buyer's concern for short-term buying criteria, but the outcome of your long-term solution must dominate the discussion. For example, "Ms. Buyer, I understand your immediate concern over price. The one thing I believe will make you feel better over the long term are the overwhelming benefits in the end result. Let's examine how this outcome will have a real impact on your business."

5. Acknowledge Price but Present to Profit

You cannot duck the price issue. It is going to come up on the sales call; it must come up. There is no need for you to get defensive about discussing price. Your strategy is to control how price is discussed. Price is a short-term, immediate-impact decision variable. Buyers naturally want to know how much something costs. Acknowledge the price of your product while maintaining the value of your product. Acknowledging your price is not agreeing it is high. Position it as an input variable in decision making, a detail to be discussed or covered in the presentation. Value is a long-term discussion. Value affects buyer profitability. The price she pays buys the product you sell, which yields the value she desires. Value, not price, must dominate the discussion.

One of the most impressive feats of role playing I have witnessed involved a discussion about a higher price for a premium product. During the presentation of features and benefits of the product, the buyer commented on the price. Without breaking stride, the salesperson said, "Isn't it amazing that we can do so much for so little more!" The conversation got back on track, and the salesperson closed the deal. He acknowledged the higher price and used it to recap the impact of his solution. He was prepared for the buyer's comment and dismissed it without getting defensive.

6. Sell All Three Dimensions of Value

If you sell product only, you open the field to other competitors. Product-only sales encourage buyers to value-strip, that is, to reduce the sale to the core-commodity aspects of your naked product. This results in a price, not a value, decision. Sell all three dimensions of value: your product, your company, and you. The same product from the same company from two different salespeople is two different solutions. Different products from different companies from different salespeople are two completely different solutions. Answer these three questions in your presentation:

- Why this product? Describe the features and benefits of the product.
- Why our company? Discuss your value-added services.
- Why me? Review your commitment to serve.

If you want the buyer to make a decision on broader issues than the core-commodity aspect of what you sell, you must infuse your conversation with all three dimensions of value: your company, your product, and yourself.

7. Sell Your Unique Selling Proposition

A major cause of price objections is buyers' failure to perceive the differences among various supply alternatives. Faced with different suppliers, buyers want to understand why one supplier is better than others. Buyers will not pay more if they do not perceive a difference (besides price), nor should they.

Gaining a preemptive selling advantage includes building a presentation around your definable and defendable differences. Respond proactively to a buyer's comment such as "You and all your competitors are in the same business." Your attitude must be, "We're in the same industry, but we're not in the same business and here's why." Own this conversation. Take the initiative on differentiation. Celebrate your differences. Use your "ten things to consider" list to support your argument. Review your USP with the buyer.

When you raise these differences early in the sales conversation, it causes the buyer to examine the various degrees of separation between you and the competition. You can achieve this with a list of feeding statements:

- "One of the things we're most proud of is . . ."
- "Customers tell us we stand out in this area . . ."
- "We really excel in this area . . ."

Any feeding statement that calls into play your definable and defendable differences will work.

8. Sell from Options Like Printers Do

Printers are masters of gaining preemptive selling advantage. On any major print job I have commissioned, the printer sold up. I would tell them that I needed a quantity of 1,000 pieces, and they would provide a quote at 1,000 pieces, 2,500 pieces, and 5,000 pieces. They offered lower prices if I would increase my order quantity; these discounts were built into my quote. The implication was crystal clear: if I wanted a cheaper price, I needed to increase my quantity. They argue that the most expensive copy to print is the first and that every copy after that is less expensive. Their built-in, preemptive way of dealing with price objections positions them to effectively field resistance.

You may not be able to offer large-quantity discounts. You can sell from options by signaling that there are two or three optional ways to purchase your solution. Some companies intentionally drive sales to the Internet so they can offer a scaled-down version of their product. Announcing different grades of a product is similar. In each case, you preempt price objections by giving the buyer a peek at negotiating options.

Some companies use decoy products to deflect price resistance and present the buyer with options. These companies offer higher-priced products to draw attention from the mainstay of their lines. I recently visited an exclusive gameroom store that sells high-end Oriental rugs and gaming equipment. They place $30,000 pool tables at the entrance. So by the time you find their main line, the $2,000 tables, you think you are getting a deal. They do the same with expensive area rugs, hanging $30,000 rugs on the walls, as stacks of $5,000 rugs invite buyers to touch and examine them. The use of these pricey decoys makes the rest of the items in the store seem *reasonable*.

9. Create a Positive Sense of Urgency

Time can displace price. You can help the buyer make a buying decision by clarifying the benefit of moving forward and contrasting it to the consequences of inertia and the cost of delay.

You create a positive sense of urgency when you provide an emotional spark to light the buyer's fuse. Reason makes people think, but emotion energizes them to act. Give the buyer rational reasons to make an emotional decision to do business with your company. Your passion, enthusiasm, and positive sense of urgency are contagious. (On the flip side, so is apathy.)

By and large, salespeople know that urgency is a powerful motivator and have misused this fact for years. For example, "Mr. Buyer, if you do not move on this today, the price is going up tomorrow, and since we only have limited inventory, I cannot guarantee the stock will be around when you want this." What makes this negative is the implied threat to the buyer: "If you do not act now, something horrible is going to happen." Most buyers react as negatively as it is presented. They stall, push back, or walk away.

On the other hand, urgency can be a powerful motivator if you use it positively. Consider it from the buyer's point of view. If you were the buyer, why would you want to move immediately on a given purchase? What is in it for the buyer? Begin with the statement, "The advantage of your moving on this now is . . ."

Here's an example: "Mr. Buyer, the advantage of your moving on this now is that we know where pricing will be going over the next thirty days, and we can save you an additional 10 percent if you decide to move on this now." This is another way of asking, "How much do you lose by waiting to buy?"

Another example is, "Because the inventory is available, we can guarantee you the delivery you want if you move on this now."

When you contrast these examples with the buy-or-else sense of urgency, you can understand why the buyer views these as positive statements. The buyer perceives it as an advantage for acting versus a disadvantage for hesitating.

Any time you introduce an element of urgency, risk is involved. If the buyer perceives a benefit to him, it is OK. If he senses you are more interested in closing the deal than solving his problem, he becomes suspicious, and you lose your credibility. Be selective when using this strategy. The positive sense of urgency works well when the buyer benefits from acting now.

PRESENT YOUR PRICE IN ITS BEST LIGHT

When is the best time to talk price? Timing is everything in sales. When presenting your price, there are some dos and don'ts. Recently my office phone rang, and on the other end, a salesperson said, "I am calling today to see if you would like to do some price shopping on your health insurance." That conversation did not last long.

"Don'ts" for Presenting Your Price

Avoid the following mistakes when discussing price:

- Don't telegraph that a cheaper price is available.
- Don't look down or stare into space when presenting price. This reflects a lack of confidence.
- Don't apologize for your price.
- Don't cover your mouth or your face.
- Don't ask if you can quote against a competitor.

- Don't ask for last look. This means the buyer will collect other price quotations and show them to you with the anticipation that you will match the lower prices.
- Don't duck when you are presenting your price.
- Don't say "list price," "manufacturer's suggested retail price," "your price," "generally what we would like to get," "what we are hoping to get," "here is our asking price," or "here is our taking price." All suggest flexibility in your pricing.

"Dos" for Presenting Your Price

Here is some good advice for discussing price:

- Do maintain steady eye contact and project confidence when discussing price.
- Do use these three words: "The price is . . ." Anything other than "the price is" sounds like there is wiggle room in your pricing.
- Do present price matter-of-factly. It is the next natural step in the process—the buyer expects to go there.
- Do explain the price without apology. You can defend it without getting defensive.
- Do frame price within the context of what the buyers get versus what they give. In other words, sell value, not price. The value comes from what your product does for the buyer, not what he pays. Think about the buyer's return on investment when presenting your price. It boosts your confidence in your product.
- Do sandwich price between benefits. For example, "For all the items we discussed, Mr. Buyer, options A, B, C, and D, the price is X, and this includes all of the value-added extras we have discussed so far." Sandwiching and summarizing benefits to smother price is an effective backdrop for the buyer to measure the true value of your package.
- Do present price with a long-term-gain focus. This paves the way for a value-over-price discussion. This arm's length view of price enables you to discuss price, cost, and value.
- Do focus on results for the buyer. Salespeople err when they focus too much on their own cost and margins versus what the product does for the buyer. If you sold something for ten dollars that the buyer could sell for fifty, how do you think she would react? She would be ecstatic.

The buyer could not care less about your costs. It is irrelevant that what you sold for ten dollars costs you only ten cents. Some salespeople focus on how much profit their company makes and consequently feel guilty about the prices they charge. This haunts them in the price discussion.

- Do lead with price to disqualify. Bring price into the conversation early when your selling instincts tell you the buyer may be unable to pay your price, and you want to qualify the buyer quickly. A word of caution here: do not delude yourself into believing you can judge a book by its cover. If you are dealing with a small business owner who dresses like the people in the shop, he may do so because he gets his hands dirty every day. Do not let his appearance mislead you.
- Do delay giving the price until you have fully explained your solution. Remember, buyers buy results. Fully explain your results before getting into pricing. Why would the buyer agree to a price without agreeing to the outcome he will experience as a result of implementing your solution and using your product? When you go to a cafeteria, you do not pay until the end, because you are charged for only what you purchase. On the other hand, if you go to a smorgasbord, you pay up-front because there is the assumption you are going for pure volume. Cafeteria pricing—pay for what you consume—means deferring your price discussion until the end because the price is irrelevant until the buyer sees what he gets for the money. For the exception to this, see the previous tip on disqualifying buyers.
- Do defer if needed. If price surfaces before you want to discuss it, defer the discussion by saying, "Before we get into price, Mr. Buyer, I want to make sure everything else is right with the package." If everything else is wrong, the price is irrelevant.
- Do start at the top. If your offer involves several pricing levels that reflect volume discounts, begin with the highest quantity pricing to demonstrate the savings involved when purchasing in large quantities. "The advantage of our pricing schedule is the savings you enjoy when purchasing in larger quantities." This is similar to the technique used by printers I mentioned earlier in this chapter.

CHAPTER SUMMARY

In the previous chapter, you learned to gain a preemptive selling advantage by shifting the buyer's focus with questions and enlarging the conversation beyond your core-commodity product. This chapter taught you how to change the conversation and enlarge the discussion beyond price. This chapter provides nine ways to enhance your presentation and several tips to present your price in its best light. Your challenge moving forward is to create a presentation that overshadows the buyer's concern for price. This will happen if you continue to stretch the buyer's time horizon and enlarge the discussion to value, not just price.

PART III

YOU CAN PERSIST WHEN THEY RESIST

I love argument, I love debate. I do not expect anyone just to sit there and agree with me, that's not their job.
—MARGARET THATCHER, FORMER PRIME MINISTER OF
THE UNITED KINGDOM

The Iron Lady earned her nickname for her steely resolve. As the only woman to have held the posts of Leader of the British Conservative Party and Prime Minister of the United Kingdom, she was no stranger to argument. She faced down labor unions, the old Soviet Union and political opponents.

Witnesses to her Parliamentary appearances saw a resolute leader, confident of her course.

Your challenge in sales may not rise to the dais on a global stage, but your confidence and resolute defense of your prices and profitability are important to your future success. Part III is about developing a stubborn resolve in protecting your margins while defending your prices. You may have done everything right to this point, but the buyer still says, "Your price is too high." What are you to do?

By reading Part III, taking notes, studying the responses, and formulating your own strategies, you will demonstrate the steely resolve of the Iron Lady and build your own reputation for confidence and competence.

10

Handling Objections

Hence to fight and conquer in all your battles is not supreme
excellence; supreme excellence consists in breaking the enemy's
resistance without fighting.

—SUN TZU, *THE ART OF WAR*

Objections need not be hand-to-hand combat. Buyers are not the enemy; it is
price-dominated thinking that you battle. The battleground is the buyer's
mind.

Objections represent a breakdown somewhere in the sales communication
process—from targeting to qualifying to presenting to closing. Years ago, I
recorded the objections salespeople brought to our seminars and discovered
that failure to qualify a prospect was the most common cause of sales resistance.
Qualifying means two things: identifying viable prospects for your business
and identifying buyers' needs, wants, and fears. Without this valuable insight
into the buyer's world, you cannot present a compelling argument for the customer to choose your solution.

Buyer resistance elicits fear and sweaty palms from most salespeople. For
them, hearing "no" is a frustrating and intimidating experience. Other salespeople boast that they enjoy objections because that is when the real selling
begins. Some sales trainers even espouse this philosophy. I do not enjoy hearing

buyers reject my ideas. This does not mean I cannot successfully respond to objections—I simply prefer to hear "yes."

This chapter is about helping you understand the nature of buyer resistance so you are less intimidated by it. This chapter covers the following topics:

- ■ Why people resist
- ■ Thirteen tips for engaging buyer resistance

At the end of this chapter, you will be able to confront resistance with a more positive attitude and better understanding of your strategy to persist when they resist.

WHY BUYERS RESIST

There are many reasons buyers resist. Here are six of the most common. Understanding them can help you proactively eliminate them in your presentation.

1. An objection is a break in your momentum. For whatever reason, the buyer has decided not to purchase your solution without some resolution. As you face resistance, it is useful to stand back and ask questions about the sales process to see if you can identify where the breakdown has occurred. The buyer may lack the money or authority to move forward. This also suggests your strategy to regain momentum.

2. People resist because they lack information. This could be a lack of information about your solution, your product, or your company. Potential buyers may misunderstand or have insufficient information to get excited enough to buy. They also may resist because they lack in-depth information about their needs. Insufficient probing by the salesperson or the buyer's own limited understanding of his own needs may contribute to this. The remedy is to educate the buyer about his needs or your solution.

3. Buyers resist because they may not need what you sell. You may be presenting something the buyer wants but does not need. This may cause an internal conflict for the buyer, and you witness it as resistance. Wants can be powerful motivators and may overshadow needs. Helping the buyer clarify his thinking may earn you the order and the buyer's respect.

4. People resist because of timing. It is not an *if* issue but a *when* issue for them. Your solution presented at a different time may elicit a more positive response from the buyer. If you sense that this is the case, ask, "Mr. Buyer, to understand where we are, is it a matter of *when* we're going to get together on this, or is it still a matter of *if* we're going to get together?" If the answer is *when*, it is a timing issue. If the answer is *if*, there is another issue. You have some selling to do. If the answer is *when*, you must agree on your follow-up strategy.

5. People resist because of attitude. A buyer may have had a bad experience with your company in the past, and it biases her opinion. Or she may be narrow-minded and feel that only her ideas matter. The buyer may have a built-in bias against technology, and even though your high-tech solution makes sense, he will not purchase it because of his bias.

With attitude-based objections, confronting the attitude head-on is your best strategy. Years ago, I conducted a sales seminar for a group of advertising salespeople. One of the salespeople shared her most difficult objection. The advertiser did not like the publisher of the newspaper and resented "putting more money in the publisher's pocket." The sales rep was stumped by this until she realized it was really more about putting money in the advertiser's pocket.

Here is how she responded: "Mr. Advertiser, I hear what you're saying. Isn't the real issue here about attracting more business to your store?" The advertiser agreed. Directly confronting the attitude objection helped her get the sale. She was respectful and assertive. She redirected the conversation to the key issue.

6. Some people resist because they lack the will to act. They may fear change. Inertia has set in; the body is at rest and they want to keep it that way. They feel little enthusiasm for your solution and see no reason to change. Their pain level with the status quo is low. The objection may surface as, "I'm happy with my current supplier (or product)." The challenge is to convince the buyer the gain is worth the pain of changing.

Acknowledge the resistance and deal with it directly. Compare the fear of change with a potential missed opportunity. For example, "Mr. Buyer, I understand that you're feeling some concern over this decision. That's understandable. Change is uncomfortable for most people. I know every great opportunity carries with it some risk. My great fear is that we have a window of opportunity here that may close if we fail to move forward. Missing it carries more risk than changing. I want you to be able to take advantage of this window of opportunity." Be sure the context of your response is positive, focusing on the advantage of moving forward. Mention the pain, but focus on the gain.

Objections mean you have experienced a break in your momentum. The immediate challenge is to understand the resistance and explore options for resolving it. You need to regain your momentum or move on to another opportunity.

TIPS FOR DEALING WITH OBJECTIONS

Whether it is a price objection, a bad past experience, inertia, or an attitude-based objection, there are common denominators for your response strategy. This list of tips will help you engage resistance more successfully.

Tip #1: You Can Anticipate Objections Without Creating Them

Preparation and study lower your risk for caving in to price objections. Preparation fixes most of the reasons you get price objections. It ensures you are calling on viable prospects who can pay for your solution. It allows time to design a presentation to convince buyers of your value.

When you anticipate objections in a positive way, you can own them as a question versus the buyer presenting them as resistance. For example, "Mr. Prospect, one of the most frequently asked questions we get about our product is . . . (this could be a common objection that buyers raise)." When you raise the objection as a question and answer it, the buyer perceives you as a fair-minded individual who is trying to hide nothing. You get to answer the question on your terms and present your product in its best light.

In my early days as a sales trainer, I created an objections file by listing every possible objection I might hear and prepared a rebuttal. I carried it with me and reviewed it often. It was a great confidence builder and made me a more effective salesman. My goal in dealing with objections was to be better prepared to deal with them than the buyer was to give them. That is a useful benchmark for you, too. Be better prepared to respond than the buyer is to resist.

Tip #2: You Can Persist Without Being a Pest

It pays to be optimistically stubborn in sales. Three out of four salespeople quit the first time a buyer says no. Another 5 percent quit on number two. The goal is not to get three nos from a buyer, but why quit before the third no? If you are discussing price, you are still in the game until you or the buyer quits.

A purchasing agent clarified for me the difference between pushy and persistent. Pushy means you are relentless because it benefits you as a salesperson.

Persistence is pressing for a decision because it benefits the buyer. You can be as persistent as you want because your goal is to help the buyer. The buyer must perceive that your motive is to make a difference, not just a deal. This means you are offering the buyer good counsel.

Tip #3: Divorce Your Ego from the Sale

It is impossible to deal with someone else's emotions when your own emotions are spiraling out of control. You can defend without getting defensive. You can argue your case without being argumentative. When the buyer rejects your price, it is not necessarily a personal attack. The buyer does not like what you are selling. Avoid defensiveness. Try to remain as objective as possible and keep it on a professional level. This is a business decision, so be as professional with the buyer as you want the buyer to be with you. The more rational your response, the more credible you sound. If you believe in your product and your company, you will be passionate, and that is a good thing. Do not let this passion devolve into contentiousness. That defeats the purpose of your conviction.

Tip #4: Use Empathy When Dealing with Objections

You can express empathy and invoke empathy. To build empathy, try to understand the objection from the buyer's perspective. Show your understanding and tell the buyer you understand his concern. Acknowledging is not agreeing; it is simply recognizing another's point of view. An in-depth understanding of his point of view helps you prepare a credible response. Demonstrating empathy relieves tension. For example, "I hear what you're saying"; "I understand your concerns"; "Yes, money is one concern."

Invoking empathy draws understanding from the buyer. It makes your answer relevant to her situation if you draw parallels between your challenges and the challenges she faces. For example, "Like you, we made a decision a long time ago to compete on our value, not our price. Because of this, each year we lose business, but we gain more than we lose, and I hope that is the case here." Certain phrases, such as "like you," invoke empathy. You want the buyer to understand your situation as much as you understand her situation. Another example would be, "Ms. Buyer, we face the same price-for-quality challenges that dominate your marketing." Again you are attempting to draw empathy from the buyer by relating your situation to what she faces in her market.

Tip #5: Be Patient with the Process and Optimistic with the Outcome

Time and emotion are major pressure points in a negotiation. If you yield to either, you will concede more than you gain. Slow down the negotiating process when it favors your position. Your empathy, passion, and enthusiasm for how your solution benefits the buyer are the only emotions you want to display. This is why professional negotiators must have their outcomes ratified by someone else. They like the time and space advantage of someone else approving the outcome. This is a compelling argument for why salespeople must confer with a higher authority before accepting a final agreement. Time and distance mitigate the impact of urgency and emotion. When buyers press you for an immediate answer, they know you will probably err in their favor.

Tip #6: Confrontation Need Not Be Combat

It is worth repeating: you can disagree with the buyer without being disagreeable. Managing rapport with buyers is essential in negotiating a win-win solution. Rapport management means you will be able to navigate the choppy waters of tough negotiations. Your goal is win-win. Respectful disagreement is not a deal killer; it is a deal preserver. Buyers respect salespeople who disagree when the buyers' positions are not in their long-term best interests. This is one reason it is imperative to keep your discussion on a professional level. Personal attacks, generalizations, and exaggerations have no place in a win-win discussion about the buyer's needs and your ability to supply the right solution.

Tip #7: Slow Down the Process

You want to give yourself the opportunity of a well-conceived response. This is different from Tip #5, which focuses on the energy of an objection. Slowing down the process can buy you time so you can think through your response strategy. Have you ever left a sales call wishing you would have said something different than you said? That is why you slow down the process.

Buyers have been on the receiving end of another's urgency ever since Eve urged Adam to take a bite of the apple. Because of this, buyers have learned from salespeople how to wield a sense of urgency to their advantage. Buyers press salespeople for a quick decision because they know salespeople who make rash price decisions often regret it later. Slow down the process to give yourself the time you need to make a prudent business decision.

Tip #8: Sometimes Buyers Think Aloud

The words flow from their mouths before the filters kick in. It could be that when the buyer says your price is too high, he is thinking out loud. The price may have surprised him but still could be within his reach. Do not overreact or get defensive. If he thinks aloud, view it as a benefit. It is a peek inside his head. I wonder how many salespeople have overreacted to a buyer's sticker shock and lowered price as a knee-jerk response to perceived resistance. This overreaction validates the buyer's surprise. It may open the door to additional haggling.

Tip #9: The Buyer May Be Testing You

The buyer wants to feel good about the price. She wants to negotiate her best deal. This may not be a true price objection but an effort to see if you will bend. This is a case where saying no to a price objection pays dividends. Saying no is like saying yes. It gets easier every time you say it. Every time you stick to your prices, you discourage the buyer's expectations that you will lower your price in the future. Most people ask for a better price when buying. It may be something as simple as, "Is that your best price?" Your response should automatically be, "We always give you our best price."

Tip #10: Clarify the Buyer's Concern and Then Buffer

Clarifying any objection is fundamentally asking "Why?" Dig deeper to understand the buyer's concern or rephrase the objection as a question. Here are several examples:

Buyer: "This is more than I wanted to pay."
Seller: "What did you want to pay?" or "Is it a question of why should you pay more than you anticipated the price to be?"

Buyer: "I do not have the budget."
Seller: "What is your budget?"

Buyer: "I had a bad experience with your company in the past."
Seller: "Please, tell me. What happened?"

Each clarifier digs deeper or restates the objection as a question. Next, you buffer. Buffering acknowledges the objection. It does not confirm it or validate it. This is similar to Tip #4 on empathy.

For example,

"I understand your concerns."
"I hear you."
"Money is *one* thing to look at with this decision."

Each of these buffers acknowledges the buyer's concern. They do not signal an agreement that the price is too high. The buffer tells the buyer he need not fear your rebuttal. You understand his concerns and will attempt to resolve them.

Tip #11: Shift the Energy

In the martial arts, you use your opponent's energy as part of your own defense. You go from the defensive mode to the offensive mode by redirecting his energy. One company I worked with wanted to consolidate a package of services involving another smaller division from their company. The larger division wanted the smaller division to discount heavily their part so the larger division could reap the profits on their end. An engineer working for the smaller division responded with, "If you do not value our services any more than that, why would you want to bundle us in the package?"

The engineer shifted the energy. He avoided defensiveness by redirecting the momentum. The spokesman from the bigger division felt the need to defend his decision to use them. Shifting the energy resulted in the smaller division getting their price.

Another example is, "If the competitor's deal is that cheap, maybe they know something about their package neither of us knows." In this example, encourage the buyer to question why the competition is so cheap. What are they leaving out? The energy has shifted from you to the buyer.

Here is a good reply: "I can't apologize for the competition's price. If they say they're cheaper, I take their word for it. I can only explain why we deliver the value in our solution." You do not want the buyer to perceive you as a smart aleck, but you do want to assertively defend your price. There is no need to apologize for your price.

Tip #12: Help the Buyer Save Face

This is especially true with a silly objection. Accept responsibility for his hesitating or misunderstanding: "Perhaps I did not give you enough information." Give him a way to gracefully say yes after the no he gave you earlier. Some salespeople recap their benefits and include some additional services to make it easier for the buyer to say yes. This is called a *hold-back position.*

When the buyer says no to your price and you say no to his request for a lower price, it is a double-rejection situation. The buyer rejects you, and you reject the buyer. Someone must give. If you plan to stand firm on your price, the buyer must concede if he wants to purchase your product. This means potentially losing face. Give the buyer an easy way out to save face and pay the higher price. Using the hold-back strategy is a face-saving opportunity. Hold back something to throw in so he feels you traded concessions.

Saving face allows the buyer to tell his peers he was able to negotiate additional value for his company. You hold the line on pricing while giving him something to brag about internally.

Tip #13: Defer the Objection

These two strategies focus on delaying the inevitable—removing the objection from the discussion until the buyer has bought fully everything else you are selling. The first strategy is to *do nothing and continue with your presentation.* Using this strategy requires instincts on your part. When a buyer raises an objection early in the conversation, he may be thinking aloud. Additionally, it does not make sense to stop and argue about price when he has not bought anything yet. The objection may not be an issue after he has heard more about your product.

I described this technique in a seminar and returned the following week to work with the same group. One of the participants told me what happened to him a few days after the first seminar. His buyer raised a price objection at the start by saying, "Here is what I have budgeted for this project." He chose to do nothing and continued with his presentation for twenty minutes. At the end of the discussion, the buyer said, "I told you up-front how much I budgeted." The salesperson responded, "Yes, I know. But, I also knew if you did not like what I presented, price would be a moot issue anyway." The strategy behind *do nothing and continue with your presentation* is to remain neutral, contain yourself nonverbally, and look beyond the objection. Continue with your presentation. Revisit price later if it becomes an issue.

The second deferral strategy is the *set-aside*. The buyer wants you to concede from the start. Unless she wants what you sell, the obstacle does not matter anyway. Acknowledge the objection initially, and ask the buyer if you can return to it at a later time. This works for price, delivery, color, packaging options, or terms.

For example, "Before we get into price (or terms), I would like to make sure our quality, product availability, and technical support are right for you. Let's set aside the price for a few minutes and revisit this later. If the quality and availability aren't right, price won't matter anyway." You can use this technique with any obstacle the buyer introduces early in the sales call.

CHAPTER SUMMARY

Buyer objections represent a breakdown in your sales momentum. For some reason, the buyer does not want to move forward. Your challenge is to understand fully the objection so you can deliver a well-conceived response. The best time to deal with an objection is never. Your preparation and proactively anticipating them allow you to craft responses before objections surface. Slowing down the process, ameliorating negative emotions, and using empathy will help you resolve the objection. There are a number of strategies you can employ to help you persist when the buyer resists. Your challenge is to be more prepared to respond to an objection than the buyer is to give it.

11

Price Precepts

> The fallacious belief that education can in some way contribute to vocational and social success has done more than most things to disrupt American education. What education can do, and perhaps all it can do, is to produce a trained mind. It is principles, and everlastingly principles, not data, not facts, not helpful hints, but principles which the rising generation requires if it is to find its way through the mazes of tomorrow.
>
> —DR. ROBERT M. HUTCHINS, FORMER CHANCELLOR OF
> THE UNIVERSITY OF CHICAGO (1945–1951)

Some salespeople fail to engage price resistance effectively because they lack a set of guidelines—an operating philosophy—for holding their ground. Developing a philosophy for dealing with price resistance begins with a set of principles (or precepts) that will guide you through the maze of responding to it.

In the previous chapter, we examined ideas for responding to objections in general. We now begin to drill down specifically on price objections. This chapter is about building a philosophy based on precepts that clarify your thinking and embolden your response strategy. These sixteen price principles will provide the foundation for building a response philosophy.

At the end of this chapter, you will be able to argue persuasively why cutting price is only one way to respond to price objections.

TOM REILLY'S PRICE PRECEPTS

A precept is a principle, rule, or maxim. The following sixteen precepts will help you formulate your sales philosophy for engaging price objections.

1. Someone Else's Opinion Does Not Make Your Price High

It is only his or her opinion, not fact. Your price is more than this buyer wants to pay. This does not mean your price is too high. One person's opinion is not market research. He is entitled to his opinion, and you are entitled to your price. When you are confident about your price, why would you let someone else's opinion confuse you? Consider his opinion as feedback, not fact. Hear it. Store it. If most buyers echo this sentiment, then you may rethink your price.

2. Lowering Price Is Only One Response to Price Objections

Just because someone raises a price objection does not mean you must lower your price. You will discover, in later chapters, dozens of alternatives to lowering your price. You win the price battle one sale at a time. Every time you hold the line on price, you are one step closer to victory in the price war. Your resilience in the face of resistance depends on your creativity and perseverance. You can persist and press your competitive advantage.

3. No One but You Cuts Your Price

You, alone, do that. Competitors may cut their price or take actions to make your job tough, but you alone make the decision to cut your price. The buyer may apply pressure, but the buyer cannot change your price. Every price reduction you give is a conscious decision on your part. The problem with blaming others is that you are not taking ownership for your success or failure. You are responsible for your prices.

4. Be a Leader, Not a Follower

When the competition does something dumb with price, you do not want to compound their mistake with your own. Playing follow-the-leader is an especially bad idea when the other person is going down the wrong path, and price-cutting is generally the wrong path. Why would you follow a competitor's lead on price cutting? That is a tacit admission your pricing strategy is flawed. Why should you get cheaper to compete with them? They need to get better to compete with you. Why would you cede your leadership position to your competition? You can appreciate how buyers will respect your decision to hold the line.

5. What Goes Up Must Come Down

Sir Isaac Newton gave us that law of gravity. He did not say what goes down must come up. When you cut the price, it means you must work hard to regain what you already had. The new price becomes the standard. Buyers remember the cheaper reference price once you have lowered your prices, and it becomes an anchor to which they cling. To move price upward, you must refight a price battle you already won in the past. Having trained in the furniture industry, I recall several manufacturers complaining the price of a sofa had been $600 forever. Once consumers locked on the number, retailers found it difficult to move up the price point.

6. Random Acts of Discounting Are Like Death by a Thousand Knife Cuts

You bleed fatally from each of those wounds. *Random* is the key word here. Changing price must be strategic and not arbitrary. Pricing is a marketing decision salespeople execute tactically. In my opinion, it should be tough for you to change prices because your actions affect your company's marketing efforts. Imagine a marketing department focused on a branding strategy for a product positioned at the top of the industry, and the sales force damages the product's image by changing the price point. This dissonance confuses the market. The most profitable companies I have worked with have a pricing authority whose primary focus is protecting margins. They are ruthless guardians of their profit.

7. Preparation Is the Key to Your Success

Whoever is better prepared for the price negotiation is most likely to emerge from the negotiation having achieved his or her goal. Scenario planning and practice will sharpen your negotiating skills. Someone will throw more money to the bottom line after the negotiation—either you or the buyer. You increase the odds your bottom line will benefit if you prepare. Just as you do not want to be outsold by a competitor, you do not want to go into a price negotiation out-prepared by the buyer. Whoever prepares better—you or the buyer—likely emerges victorious. If you plan for a win-win outcome, you and the buyer will leave the negotiation with a sense of equity.

8. Never Assume Your Price Is Too High: Maybe the Buyer's Expectations Are Too Low

Do not let the buyer reduce your package or minimize your approach to the market. Your company has created a bundle of value to appeal to a certain group of buyers called a *segment*. A segment is a group of customers who share common needs. If the person you are dealing with is outside that segment, the buyer is wrong, not your product. Why would you limit your potential by playing down to their expectations? If buyers value-strip your package, they are wrong for you. You have a choice for when to walk. Sticker shock is another manifestation of unrealistic expectations on behalf of the buyer. The buyer's lack of knowledge about real-world pricing does not make your price wrong. It suggests the buyer is uninformed.

9. Never Assume Your Price Is Too High: Maybe the Competition Is Desperate

This is similar to price precept 4—do not compound a competitor's mistake. When the competition offers desperate pricing, let the buyer see the desperation. Do not mask it by joining the madness. How can you benefit from the competition's desperation if you provide cover for their actions? Failing to cut your price amplifies the competition's desperate move. When the competition admits they have been overcharging the buyer, let that sink in. When you hold the line and they cave in, the competitor's strategy will backfire on them. Short term, you may lose a sale because of their desperation pricing, but you will gain in the long run. How long can a competitor operate with desperation pricing? Their lack of confidence in their value is a differentiator for you.

10. Never Assume Your Price Is Too High: Maybe the Buyer Is Misleading You

Do some buyers lie? Yes. These are predatory price shoppers—those who will do anything to drive down the price of things. A buyer who tells you he or she can buy something cheaper somewhere else may be uttering nothing more than wishful thinking. I do not want you to develop a negative or adversarial attitude toward buyers. I simply want to alert you to this possibility so you can safeguard your profit. When selling to this type of buyer, you must choose whether or not the hassle is worth the sale.

11. People Ask for More in a Negotiation than They Reasonably Expect to Receive

This is the unwritten law of negotiating. When you make a major purchase, do you accept the first price that comes your way, or has experience taught you to drag your feet? Most of us drag our feet because salespeople have reinforced this behavior in the past by dropping their prices. Buyers believe if they ask for more than they hope to get, they will end up closer to their target number. If you know this is coming, you are better equipped to deal with it.

12. First, Buyers Test Your Price, Then They Test Your Resolve

They want to find out if you are serious about your pricing. Acting courageously in the face of price resistance depends on how prepared you are for the request. There is an element of risk when you say no to a price objection. This is when you need to reach deep into yourself for the resolve to hold the line. It helps if you gain a preemptive selling advantage and master the response strategies detailed in later chapters. You will be in a stronger position to resist the impulse to cut price. The buyer will witness your resolve and confidence. They will feel better about your price, knowing you did not budge.

13. Just Say No

You may not be able to dissuade buyers from asking for a cheaper price, but you can influence their expectations as to whether they will actually get the cheaper price. Buyers will ask for a lower price. It is their job. Your job is to say no. If you say no often enough, they may stop asking for a cheaper price. At a minimum, you can lower their expectations that you will relent on price.

I was talking with a friend who is a vice president of sales. He told me the most effective response to price objections his salespeople used was to "say no." Imagine the power of a simple no.

"Can you give me a better price?"
"No. This is our price."

"Will you work with us on pricing?"
"No. We would be thrilled to work with you any way we can. This is the price."

"Can you sharpen your pencil a bit on your prices?"

"No. I can sharpen my pencil, but it won't affect our prices."

None of these is intended to be flippant, and you will want to avoid that perception.

14. Salespeople Cut Price Because They Can

The number one reason salespeople cut price is that they can. As I mentioned earlier in this book, I have long argued that salespeople should not have pricing authority, because I have witnessed discounts given to buyers indiscriminately. You would be surprised at the number of salespeople who have confided in me their relief that they cannot give discounts. A young sales rep told me, "When I had price authority, I spent most of my time figuring a way to shave pennies off my price. Since I cannot change our prices, I spend all of my time selling our value."

I was training a group of advertising salespeople for an industry trade publication. The salespeople confided in me that their company's no-discount policy was a relief. Everyone in their industry now knew the price was not flexible. It was a fait accompli—they never had to haggle over price.

15. Buyers Want Equity

As I have stated many times in this book, buyers want to feel they are getting as good as they are giving. They want to know that what they purchase will return benefits in measure to what they give up to acquire it. Equity is a powerful motivator. It is a foundation for the win-win philosophy. Buyers who feel they gave better than they got will seek out a different supplier. Buyers who get as good as they give will seek ways to do more business with their business partners. Equity is a two-way street. You feel better about the outcome, too. If you reflect on a sale you made when you gave better than you got, you probably resented the business. That is the effect of inequity.

16. Last Look Is Fool's Gold

Sometimes a buyer says to a sales rep, "If nothing else, we will give you a last look." Or the salesperson may ask out of desperation, "Can I at least have last look?" This is fool's gold. When you agree to last look, you have fundamentally told the buyer there is room left in your pricing to negotiate.

Additionally, the buyer has admitted he operates without scruples because he is willing to show you another supplier's deal so he can leverage a better price from you. Do you think he will offer last look to your competitors, too? Last look is not what it promises to be. The best response to last look comes from a salesman who attended one of my seminars. When confronted with a last look opportunity, he responds, "Why do I need last look when I give my best deal from the start?"

CHAPTER SUMMARY

It is important to develop a sales philosophy for engaging price resistance. Buyers want equity. Sellers want equity. When there is a breakdown in equity, resentment follows. The time to develop a philosophy about pricing is before the negotiation, not during it. Your understanding of the sixteen precepts is a foundation upon which you can build a response strategy. Your challenge moving forward is to develop and demonstrate the courage of your convictions.

12

Four-Step Price Objections Response Model™

It's easy to say what you're going to do. The hard thing is figuring out what you're not going to do.

—MICHAEL DELL, FOUNDER OF DELL INC.
(*WALL STREET JOURNAL*, JANUARY 31, 1995)

Dell is describing the power of discernment. In business, it is important to know what to do, but it is imperative to know what not to do. Discernment helps salespeople discover what the buyer is really saying with, "Your price is too high." This generic money objection can mean several things: no money, no authority to make a decision, the timing is wrong, a competitor is cheaper, or no desire to buy. The challenge is to sift through the wording to identify the real objection.

This chapter is about identifying the true objection so you can respond appropriately. You can discern the real objection by following the Four-Step Price Objections Response Model™. Here are the main topics contained in the model and covered in this chapter:

- Clarifying and identifying the motivation behind the price objection
- Classifying the price objection into one of five types of money objections

■ Thinking through your response strategy
■ Responding to the five types of money objections

At the end of this chapter, you will be able to successfully overcome price resistance and never be at a loss when the buyer says, "Your price is too high."

USING THE FOUR-STEP PRICE OBJECTIONS RESPONSE MODEL

Has the buyer ever stunned you with a price objection? If so, you are on the road to recovery with the Four-Step Price Objections Response. Dealing with price objections is a four-step process:

1. Clarify the objection.
2. Classify the objection.
3. Decide how to respond.
4. Respond. (Refer to Table 12.1.)

"Your price is too high." "I can get this cheaper somewhere else." "I don't have the budget." "I must put this out for bid." "I don't want to pay that much." Even though these sound like price objections, each is a different type of money objection. Your challenge is to determine which type of money objection the buyer is giving you. Most salespeople react emotionally to a price objection, which interferes with their resolving it. This model will steady your response.

STEP ONE: CLARIFY THE OBJECTION

People object to price for various reasons: they may lack the money, authority, or confidence in your product; they may feel guilty spending that much money on themselves; they may be frugal or even cheap; they may be cautious; or they may reject the price because they think it is the right thing to do. A knee-jerk reaction to price is a different objection than one from a buyer who does not perceive your value.

Clarifying gives you time to collect your thoughts and move from an emotional reaction to a well-conceived response. Slow down the negotiating process and seek to understand the motivation behind the objection because that motivation is your real challenge. Clarifying is digging deeper and asking why

Table 12.1 Four-Step Price Objections Response Model™

Objection	"Your price is too high."	"I can buy this cheaper somewhere else."	"I don't have that much in my budget."	"I must put this out for bid."
Step One: Clarify	Slow down the conversation to understand the objection. Dig deeper to get to the *why*, the motivating force: Clarify, quantify, or restate the objection as a question.	**Ask the buyer:** "Would you please elaborate?" "What did you think the price would be?" "Is this an apples-to-apples comparison?" "Are you talking about acquisition price or ownership costs?" "When you say we're higher, could you be more specific?" **Ask yourself:** "Is this a price or package objection?" "Is this an information or attitude objection?" "Is money at the core of this?"		
Step Two: Classify	Once you understand the objection, classify it into one of five types of money objections: price, cost, value, game, or procedure.	**Price:** This includes low expectations, lack of budget, no money, sticker shock, knee-jerk reaction, or an arbitrary rejection of any price. **Cost:** This is driven by an overall cost-reduction initiative or desire to achieve operational efficiency. **Value:** The buyer does not perceive your value or the difference between you and the competition. **Game:** This includes any effort by the buyer to drive down the selling price. **Procedure:** A policy mandates competitive bids or compliance to contract purchasing.		

Step Three: Decide	Decide whether you will discount or respond with a different strategy.	**Ask yourself:** "How much pressure is the buyer feeling to buy?" "Can we sell this somewhere else at our price?" "What are the long-term consequences of our discounting?" "If we discount, what will we ask for in return?" "Other than money, what can we concede?"
Step Four: Respond	Having considered your options, respond after thoughtful preparation.	**Price:** For a lack of money, help the buyer find the money. If it is a lack of information, educate the buyer about prices. **Cost:** Demonstrate how your product will help the buyer maximize his profitability through efficiency or expansion. **Value:** Reiterate your value added or demonstrate key differences between you and the competition. **Game:** Recognize it for what it is. Your response depends on the game. **Procedure:** Become part of the recognized solution provider. Can you negotiate versus bid?

so you can respond to the right objection by focusing on the buyer's true motivation. These questions are examples of clarifiers:

■ What did you anticipate the price to be?
■ Are we talking an apples-to-apples comparison here?
■ Are you talking about the acquisition price or the total cost of ownership of this product?
■ When you say we are higher, could you elaborate, please?
■ When you say we are higher, compared to what?

Notice I use the word *higher* instead of *high*. *Higher* implies the buyer is comparing it to something else, which opens the door for you to explain your value.

You can check the buyer's sincerity when you clarify with the following questions:

■ Is price your only reason for hesitating?
■ If we resolve this price issue, are you prepared to move forward?

The buyer's answer will help you determine if the objection is real or a red herring. A red herring is something the other person uses to distract you or mislead you. For example, the buyer may not have the authority to approve your higher price, so to save face, the buyer may object to your price instead of telling you he lacks the authority. Price objections are easy objections to give because they are the least personal, and salespeople expect to hear them. A buyer can reject your price but still act as if he wants to do business with you. This enables the buyer to leave open the door for future business opportunities with you. By rejecting your price, the buyer can act as if everything else is fine, but the price is the only issue.

Skilled salespeople clarify as a way to turn the objection into a question. This enables the salesperson to answer the objection as a question. Reframing the objection as a question means you own the question and the buyer feels no need to defend it—these are your words. For example,

■ So, is it a question of how our price for this package is fair?
■ Are you really asking about the value we deliver for the price we charge?
■ The fact that you have raised the subject of money suggests to me you want to feel secure that this is the best value. Is that true?

In the previous chapter, I talked about the importance of buffering or acknowledging an objection. This would be a good place to use a buffering statement like one of the following:

- I know price is one thing you study as part of your overall profitability on this project.
- I understand your budget concerns.
- Money is one thing to look at.

These buffers do not confirm the price is too high. They acknowledge the objection and redirect it. Price is not the most important factor, just one. This encourages the buyer to consider it for what it is—one factor! Your acknowledgement that it is one factor demonstrates empathy and understanding without yielding on your position that your solution is the better solution.

Once you understand why the buyer resists your price, you can further clarify the objection by asking yourself these questions:

- Is it a price objection or a package objection?
- Is it a price objection or a value objection?
- Is it a price objection or a lack-of-money objection?
- Is it a price objection or a lack-of-information objection?
- Is it a price objection or a stall for some other reason?

Understanding the buyer's motivation is necessary to advance to step two.

STEP TWO: CLASSIFY THE OBJECTION

All price objections are different, yet they share one common denominator—money. Once you understand the nature of the objection, you can classify it into one of five types of money objections: price, cost, value, game, or procedure.

▪ **Price-based money objections.** There are three varieties of price-based money objections. One is low expectations, which includes sticker shock or a lack of information about the price of things. The second is a lack of money or budgetary constraints. The third variety of price-based money objections is attitudinal—a knee-jerk or arbitrary rejection of your price, reflecting an attitude or bias.

■ **Cost-based money objections.** These are driven by a cost-reduction initiative or desire to achieve operational and logistical efficiency in the organization. The buyer is responding to this initiative. Of the five types of money objections, these may be the easiest to deal with if you are able to demonstrate how your product helps the buyer achieve operational efficiency and lower costs.

■ **Value-based money objections.** There are two varieties of value-based money objections. One is a lack of differentiation. The buyer does not perceive the differences between you and the competition. Consequently, she does not want to pay more to work with you. The other is a perceived lack of equity. The buyer does not appreciate the value in your proposition. Again, she does not see a reason to pay more for your solution. The buyer may have the money but sees no reason to exchange it for your solution. She feels that she is giving more than she will receive.

■ **Game-based money objections.** A game is any gambit, maneuver, or ploy a buyer uses to drive down the selling price. Games are carefully planned and executed strategies. This is where your negotiating skills intervene to help you maintain a win-win focus. Games include the stiff-arm (take it or leave it); competitive stooge (someone else is cheaper); and feigned outrage (you're killing me with that price).

■ **Procedural-based money objections.** These come about in response to policy mandates for competitive bids or compliance to purchasing contracts. These are the toughest to deal with because you must be part of the process to compete.

Identifying the true nature of these five types of money objections and classifying price objections accordingly will help you design your response strategy.

STEP THREE: DECIDE HOW YOU WILL RESPOND

Now, you must decide whether you will discount, and if not, how to respond to the price resistance. Having time to think is the most compelling reason to slow down the negotiating process. You want the benefit of a well-conceived strategy. Ask yourself these questions:

■ How much pressure is the buyer feeling to buy from us?
■ Could we sell this somewhere else at a higher price?

- What are the long-term consequences, positive and negative, of discounting?
- How does this affect our other business?
- If we discount, what will we ask for in return?
- Other than money, are there other concessions we can trade?

The answers to these questions will help guide your thoughts in planning your response strategy.

STEP FOUR: RESPOND TO THE MONEY OBJECTION

In this section, I will preview these response strategies and drill down on each of them in the next five chapters.

■ **Price-based money objections.** These require information, money, and assertive responses. If the main problem is a lack of information about the price, educate the buyer. What collateral support materials can you use to reinforce your position? Most price objections fit this category; buyers do not know the price of things. This approach works well for sticker shock. If the issue is a lack of money, help the buyer find money. What type of creative financing options do you offer? Would terms help? If it is an attitudinal price objection, respond assertively and respectfully. You might be responding to the buyer who says, "We never pay list price for anything." Your response may be blunter than your typical way of engaging price objections and that is OK.

■ **Cost-based money objections.** These types of objections demand proof of lower operating expense throughout the life cycle of your solution. You must demonstrate how your solution will help the buyer maximize profitability through efficiency and expansion or leverage and growth. In either case, you will shift the focus to the lower cost of ownership and the long-term benefits of using your product.

■ **Value-based money objections.** These objections call for more information. Demonstrate key differences between you and the competition or reiterate your value added. The buyer lacks information and the conviction that your solution is more valuable and different than the competition or that your solution is worth the price.

▪ **Game-based money objections.** These money objections test your negotiation skills. If the buyer is playing a game, do not fall for it. See it for what it is—a game. Realizing it is a game strips it of its power over you. Your specific response depends on the game. You will be able to craft a response strategy after reading the next few chapters.

▪ **Procedural-based money objections.** These objections require patient persistence. Successfully engaging these objections takes time. You may need to pursue a policy change at a higher-level decision maker, become a recognized solution provider, or engage in a bidding process. You could also ask the buyer, "What do you hope to accomplish with a bid you could not get working with us one-on-one?" Going for a negotiated settlement is preferable to a bid.

CHAPTER SUMMARY

The Four-Step Price Objections Response Model™ is designed to help you persist when buyers resist and stand your ground in the face of price objections. This model steers you away from a knee-jerk reaction on your part to a well-conceived and patient response to the resistance. You will clarify the objection, classify it as one of five types of money objections; think through your response strategy, and respond. No two price objections are alike. Your response will depend on the nature of the objection. Your challenge moving forward is to commit this model to memory so you can apply it spontaneously and naturally as you encounter resistance.

13

Responding to Price-Based Money Objections

All animals are equal, but some animals are more equal than others.
—GEORGE ORWELL, *ANIMAL FARM*

Price shoppers appear single-minded in their approach to buying. They want the cheapest price for a good or service that will meet their needs. Sometimes they want the best product for the least amount of money. Other times, they may just want a product that is cheap but will still do the job. All price shoppers are not created equal nor are all price objections. Your job, as pointed out in the last chapter, is to determine the nature of the price objection and the underlying motivation.

This chapter is the first of five that deal with specific types of money objections introduced in the previous chapter. Here are the topics covered in this chapter:

- Three types of price-based money objections
- Fourteen ways to respond to these three price-based objections

By studying these concepts and integrating them into your response strategy, you will be able to engage price-based objections confidently and effectively.

THE THREE SUBTYPES OF PRICE-BASED MONEY OBJECTIONS

Price-based money objections include three subtypes of objections: lack of information, lack of money, and attitudinal. You will find different responses to each of these objections in this chapter. Read them and learn them, with a caveat: do not memorize these responses verbatim. Learn the concept, understand the response, and reframe it to sound like you, not the book. As you make it your own, it becomes and sounds more natural and spontaneous. Rote, automatic responses to price objections sound clichéd. Planned need not mean canned. It is your objection to deal with and your response to give.

LACK-OF-INFORMATION OBJECTIONS

The first type of price-based money objection comes from the buyer's lack of information. You witness this when the buyer expects unrealistically low prices or experiences sticker shock. The buyer does not expect to pay the higher price, because he lacks sufficient information. He may say any of the following:

- ▪ "Wow! I didn't know that these things cost that much."
- ▪ "That's more than I expected to spend for this."

Your response strategy is to educate the buyer. These four responses approach the objection differently.

Bring the Buyer up to Speed

Simply inform the buyer that this is the cost of the product. You may use support material to shore up your argument. Your response may sound like this: "I've had a number of first-time buyers who were a little surprised at first look. Once we explained our pricing to them and what goes into it, they understood."

The first sentence is a buffer that exonerates the buyer's uninformed objection. He realizes others have misunderstood at first. This helps the buyer save face. This buffer makes it easier for the buyer to accept your response.

Give the Buyer Permission to Buy Your Value-Added Solution

There are times a buyer needs to know it is OK to pay more than he anticipated. You must encourage and reassure the buyer. This response works well with a buyer who has worked hard and deserves the best. He needs reassurance it is OK to spend the money.

For example, if you sell a packaging solution, your response may sound like, "Mr. Buyer, you've invested significantly in the development of your product. You start with the best quality raw materials and run them through a top-quality manufacturing process. Wouldn't it make sense to invest in a packaging solution that reflects the quality of your total solution?"

It is advisable for this buyer to pay more for a packaging solution because of the other investments he made. You are telling him he has earned the right to buy the best. You may notice the use of the analogy in this response statement. Drawing an analogy to other areas where he has invested money in quality gives him permission to spend more on your solution. This response strategy also works well for a buyer who operates frugally in all areas. This may be the *one* area in which he needs to be more extravagant. Build your argument around the concept that spending more is a prudent decision.

Sell the Investment Value of Your Solution

If the buyer views your product as an expense rather than an investment, she is focusing more on the money leaving her. Buyers with an expense mindset buy the least and cheapest they can live with. If you reshape the buyer's perception of your product as an investment, not an expense, she thinks about the money returning to her. You are selling conceptually the best solution versus the cheapest solution. You are also selling the buyer on the concept that she is not spending money with you or for the given product but investing in her company. For example, "Ms. Buyer, I am not suggesting that you spend money on our product, I am recommending that you invest money in your business by using our product. This is an investment for you, not an expense. You are investing in our solution for the return you're seeking for your business."

This may be an investment in her product quality, her packaging, or her ability to serve her customer better. Shift the buyer's focus from the present to the future—from input to outcome. As an investment, you are focusing the buyer on the long term, which paves the way for you to discuss the return on investment in your solution.

Switch the Reference Price

Use this strategy with the buyer who attempts to minimize your product by saying, "It is just a (fill in the blank here)." This may be a full-blown attempt to trivialize your product by demeaning its importance and commoditizing it. This tactic comes from the attitude that if he can cheapen your image, you will lower your price. Another possibility is that the buyer believes purchasing your type of product is no big deal and assigns little importance to it. Informing is your best response strategy.

I read about a small brewer of specialty beers who avoided direct price comparisons with mass-market beers by comparing his product to fine wines. He knew that wine customers were accustomed to paying more for a better label. This brewer switched the product reference price to an entirely different competitor: "Mr. Buyer, I know it is tempting to reduce a product to its core function. The problem with reducing our solution to its naked product is that leaves many of your needs exposed. This ignores all the special reasons you want to work with us. It is like saying there's nothing special about your needs. Do you really believe that?"

LACK-OF-MONEY PRICE OBJECTIONS

This second type of price-based money objection is self-explanatory. Remember, the buyer's lack of budget or funding does not make your price high. Can you help the buyer find the money or justify an increase in his budget? These five response strategies give you flexibility in responding to this objection.

Add Value or Bundle

Since you have decided against cutting the price, consider building the package. Building the package, sometimes called *bundling*, shifts the focus from price to package. The package brings the value the buyer wants and needs. That is the conversation you want to have with the buyer. Building the package increases perceived value and creates equity in the buyer's mind. The buyer may offer suggestions for where she would like you to add value or enhance the package. "Ms. Buyer, if you have a real concern about the relationship between our price and the package, maybe there's a way we can build more value into the package so you feel more comfortable with the price."

Subtract Value or Unbundle

This is the opposite of the previous strategy. With this response, you focus on what you need to remove from the package to meet the price the buyer is willing to pay. Advise the buyer that the only way for you to lower your price is to strip value from your package. The importance of this response is the shock value of telling the buyer what it takes to lower your price. "Ms. Buyer, if your primary concern is price, maybe there is a way for us to remove some of the value from our solution to meet the price you are willing to pay."

This is a legitimate way to change your price. Perhaps you can strip value or recommend a different, albeit less expensive, alternative. Value substitution is another option. Switch one product, or grade of product, for another. Another variation is providing a lower quantity of the solution. The buyer may settle for a quantity of ten products versus twelve products. You legitimize your changing the price by changing the package.

The advantage of having more than one value proposition is that you can offer a "price-shopper special" without damaging your lead brand. The price-shopper special is a value-stripped alternative geared to price-conscious buyers. Some companies call this a *flanking-brand strategy*. It is a similar product that will meet the buyer's most basic needs.

Restructure the Deal

Restructuring the deal gives the buyer a different way to look at your price—another decision to make. There is no such thing as a bad deal, just bad structure. Say to the buyer: "Mr. Buyer, somewhere in here I know is a good deal for both of us if we are just willing to hang in here long enough to find it. Maybe there's a way for us to restructure our financing or delivery to reflect your budget constraints."

Seek common ground. Your buyer may need a different deal to present to a higher buying authority. Is there another way to finance your idea? Is there another way to package your offer? You might be able to change the terms of the agreement or adjust the billing cycle for your buyer. One idea for changing terms is to get the buyer to pay before delivery or offer extended terms and delayed billing to fit his budget constraints. Some companies use accelerated or variable payment schedules that parallel cash flow variances in the buyer's business. If his business is seasonal, adjust your payment to reflect periods of higher or lower cash flow.

Buy Dissonance

Buying dissonance spotlights the disconnect between what the buyer says and does. He may tell you his needs are special but opts for a cheaper, generic solution. He may claim the solution is mission critical but chooses a cheaper alternative. In this disconnect lies the seed for a compelling rebuttal. You can emphasize the threat of loss when purchasing a cheaper alternative: "Mr. Buyer, is the quality you are willing to pay for consistent with your immediate needs and your long-term objectives?"

Here are some product-specific examples:

- If you sell furniture: "Is the quality of the furniture you are willing to pay for consistent with the image you want to project?"
- If you sell industrial tubing: "Is the quality of the tubing you are willing to purchase consistent with the quality of material that passes through it?"
- If you sell construction tools: "Is the quality of tools you are willing to pay for consistent with the quality of workers for whom you are buying the tools?"

Demonstrate that his purchasing objectives conflict with the price he wants to pay. This dissonance motivates the buyer to rethink his decision to buy cheap. It also demonstrates you have his best interest in mind. You may return to a previous response strategy and give the buyer permission to pay more than he anticipated.

Point Out the Double-Edged Sword

This response strategy gives you an opportunity to reinforce your total value. Appeal to the buyer's common sense. If you cut price, you must cut something from your package. This is closely related to value subtraction. Use your value-in-purchasing list and detail the value added you must remove to justify this price cut. "When people ask us to cut our price, it's really a double-edged sword for us. If we swing the sword one way to cut price, we must swing it in the other direction to cut something from our package to justify the price cut. The problem is that whatever we cut from our value proposition is the reason why people want to do business with us. That is why it is a double-edged sword."

ATTITUDINAL PRICE OBJECTIONS

The third type of price-based money objection comes from a buyer who automatically and arbitrarily rejects your price. This knee-jerk reaction expresses several attitudes about price. For example,

- "I never pay asking price for anything."
- "You owe me a quantity discount."
- "Sellers always leave room to negotiate."

The foundation for this type of objection is the buyer's attitude that he deserves a cheaper price and you must relent on your price. These five responses will help you craft a response.

Highest-Volume Discount Response

Some buyers never believe that they get the best available deal. This is especially true of small business owners who believe others get a better price than they. This response is designed for the buyer who fears everyone else gets a better deal. "Mr. Buyer, I understand your request for a lower price. Here is our dilemma. The price we quoted you is exactly the same price we charge our highest volume user. How can we offer you a lower price than we offer our highest volume customer? That's not good business. Besides, if we started discounting our prices now, wouldn't you wonder why we didn't do this before you asked for a lower price? What would this do to our trust bond?"

Some buyers are reassured by the fact that no one gets a cheaper price than they. The auto industry created a sales model called the *no-dicker sticker*. There is one price, and everyone pays it. This eliminates haggling. It is a take-it-or-leave-it offer. Most automobile buyers report they like the no-haggle model of buying. It restores their confidence in the price they pay. Some people will pay more if they are convinced it is the best deal available and no one else gets a better deal.

Exponential Advantage of Volume

Most buyers believe they should pay a lower price if they purchase in volume. Many sellers promote this thinking, and there is a solid operations argument to support this perspective. The efficiencies of scale pose a tempting argument for passing along savings to customers.

On the other hand, where is it written that selling a higher volume mandates a lower price? Some businesses operate this way, but why? What rule compels you to embrace this thinking? I believe we should challenge this thinking with a different argument—one that most people have never considered. Answer these questions:

- When you sell more of something, does your quality suffer?
- When you sell more of something, does your service falter?
- When you sell more of something, does your value diminish?

Why should your price drop if your quality, service, and value meet or exceed the buyer's expectations? "Mr. Buyer, the quality of what we sell and our service level are not diminished by the quantity we sell. When you buy more, we do not discount, because we are convinced there is an exponential advantage to your owning this product. The more of our product you use, the greater the benefit."

The argument of exponential advantage is a different way to view quantity purchases. If the buyer is convinced of your value, there is an exponential benefit of his using more of what you sell. One example of exponential advantage is custom manufacturing. As the company manufactures more of the custom product, the quality generally gets better. They become more efficient and effective at production. Why should the price go down as the quality gets better? That is the benefit of continuous improvement: customers get a better product, and the seller earns more profit. The same argument can be made for increasingly good service levels. The more you sell, the better you get at serving customers. Again, why should the price go down?

There is an inherent advantage to purchasing in large quantities and standardizing on a supplier or product. There is a logistics benefit to consolidating purchasing because the buyer issues fewer purchase orders to one supplier. There is a functional benefit to employees standardizing on one product relative to training, maintenance, repair, and usage. This point of view is meant to challenge your automatic response to the greater quantity argument. The quantity discount is so imprinted in the market psyche that most buyers and sellers consider it a fait accompli. Challenge this thinking with the leverageable value of your product in greater quantities. How does your product and company offer the buyer an exponential advantage?

Sense of Fairness

Psychologists believe that most people embrace a sense-of-fairness philosophy. This means they want to treat others fairly and be treated fairly. Appealing to the buyers' sense of fairness demonstrates you are looking out for them. This response reassures the buyer you protect them with your pricing strategy. "Every year we reinvest in research and development to create more value for our customers. It is unfair to our current partners for us to discount our products for someone else when they are as heavily invested in our future as we are.

You will be able to rest assured that if you partner with us we will honor that commitment by not lowering our prices to someone else for an order."

Reassure the buyer you protect them by protecting your price. No one will get a better deal than your buyer, and you will continue to innovate, which means he will reap the benefits of this innovation. Another way to appeal to the sense of fairness is to demonstrate your loyalty to existing customers. For example: "Mr. Buyer, we believe we partner with some pretty sharp business-people. They like our quality and service. They appreciate our value. And they pay our price. For us to lower our price for you is like saying that all of those customers made a bad decision to do business with us. We won't say that about our customers. We certainly wouldn't say that about you if you buy from us."

Reject the Offer

There are times to reject an offer and walk because you and the buyer cannot agree on price. If the buyer never witnesses your walking point, she will continue to ask for more concessions. Knowing and demonstrating your walking point sends a powerful message to the buyer that you have reached the end of the negotiating session. You can exit gracefully. For example: "It has been our experience that we are better off to reject a price now than to resent the business later. This way we can part friends and leave the door open for future business."

If the buyer's price request represents unprofitable business for your company, you could say, "Would you really want to do business with us if we took this deal?" It is a nice way for you to say no to the lower price request. It is also possible when the buyer senses you are ready to walk, she will change her mind. She may have been testing you. Knowing a seller has reached the walking point reassures the buyer this is the best deal available.

Give It Back to the Buyer

This is an unexpected and powerful technique for dealing with price objections. Salespeople, for years, have convinced buyers that if they do not buy now, something negative is going to happen—a sort of doomsday scenario. This response does the opposite. Encourage the buyer to think about it.

The buyer says, "I don't know. The price is higher than I want to pay."

Attempt to deal with it, and if nothing seems to work, offer this response, "Do you really need to say no to our price right now?"

Buyers typically respond, "No, not really."

"Then, let me offer this suggestion. If you don't need to say no right now, think about it for a few days, and let's talk one more time. When you say no to our price, you're also saying no to all those reasons you want to work with us."

This shift in momentum will surprise the buyer, and you may be able to resurrect what appears to be a dead sale. The last thing the buyer expects is your telling him to think about it. Encourage the buyer to take time to make a good buying decision. This is a complete reversal of the sense-of-urgency close salespeople use.

CHAPTER SUMMARY

Price-based money objections surface as a lack of information, lack of funding, or attitudinal resistance. Each requires a different response strategy. You learned fourteen response strategies to the three types of price-based money objections. Studying these strategies and integrating them into your responses will equip you to respond effectively to this type of money objection.

14

Responding to Cost-Based Money Objections

Looking only at a product's acquisition cost is like looking only at the tip of an iceberg. Below the surface of the acquisition cost lie the treacherous costs of owning and using the product.

—DR. EBERHARD SCHEUING, ISM PROFESSOR OF PURCHASING AND SUPPLY
LEADERSHIP EMERITUS AT ST. JOHN'S UNIVERSITY, *VALUE-ADDED PURCHASING*

Price shoppers look at price, not cost. Cost is bigger than price and therein lies the challenge for salespeople. Looking deeper than surface price requires extra effort. Buyers who are obsessed on price only, the tip of the iceberg, are like the captain of the *Titanic*, as they are drawn to the thing that could sink their efforts at a good solution.

You can change the buyer's opinion and respond effectively to cost-based money objections. This chapter will help you do this by covering the following topics:

- The driving forces behind this objection
- Five ways to respond to the cost-based objection

By studying these concepts and integrating them into your response strategy, you will be able to engage confidently and effectively cost-based money objections.

DRIVING FORCES BEHIND COST-BASED MONEY OBJECTIONS

This type of money objection is different from the price-based money objections in the previous chapter. Price is about acquisition; cost is about ownership and usage. *Price* describes the money that buyers exchange to acquire something. *Cost* describes what buyers invest to own, operate, transform, or resell something. Price is a short-term decision variable; cost is a long-term decision variable. Sometimes it is referred to as total cost of ownership (TCO) or life cycle costs. Buyers who offer a cost-based money objection intend to lower operating costs.

Maybe management has told purchasing to reduce costs, and purchasing interprets this as finding the cheapest price for something. Maybe your buyer's customers are applying pressure to your buyer for a cheaper price, and he in turn wants to pass it along to you. In reality, the buyer needs a way to compete profitably in one of his price-sensitive accounts. You may be hearing a request, masked as a price objection, so your buyer can throw more money to the bottom line for shareholders.

Cost-based money objections represent a way for the buyer to become more operationally efficient and fiscally responsible. This is not the same motivation that drives the buyer who is experiencing sticker shock or holds an opinion he never pays asking price for anything. Understanding the driving forces behind the objections versus accepting them at face value provides you with insight in how to develop your response strategy.

STRATEGIES FOR RESPONDING TO COST-BASED MONEY OBJECTIONS

Money is a better conversation to have with buyers than price. Long-term is better than short-term. These five response strategies will help you change the conversation using these two facts and ultimately the buyer's mind.

Stretch the Buyer's Time Horizon

Cost is a broader discussion than price. Price refers specifically to acquisition while cost refers to ownership. Ownership lasts longer than acquisition. Time horizon is a key difference between a price shopper and a cost shopper. If your solution delivers a positive financial impact, you can deal effectively with this type of money objection. This response strategy is similar to a probing question from Chapter 8. Stretch the buyer's time horizon for using and owning your product: "If you were to look back on this decision twelve or eighteen months from now and say you made a great decision to go with our solution, on what criteria would you make that judgment?" Or, you could ask, "What does a successful outcome look like to you?"

Pause and let the buyer's response sink in. Rarely will price be the issue. You will hear these types of answers:

- "We received a better quality solution."
- "The solution really performed."
- "We got product as we needed it."
- "We got the technical support when we needed it most."

With a cost-based money objection, your immediate objective is to stretch the time horizon so the buyer will understand and appreciate your long-term value. Cost-based shoppers are willing to look beyond the acquisition point to the total cost of ownership and the impact of your solution.

Financially Justify

The first rule of financially justifying a sale is to focus only on the price difference. The price difference could be the difference in pricing between your product or service and the competition's product or service. It could be the difference between your price and what the buyer anticipated or budgeted to spend. By focusing only on the difference, you have a smaller and more manageable number to justify. For example, if your price is $10,000 and the other price is $9,000, you need to justify only the $1,000 difference. This redirects the buyer to a smaller number.

There are two ways to financially justify a price: miniaturizing and fractionalizing. *Miniaturizing* is reducing the price to a small, manageable, and sometimes ridiculous number—cost per use, cost per application, cost per hour, or cost per unit. It is presenting your price in a way that makes it easy for the buyer to digest. For example, assume you are working with a $1,000 price differential between your price and a competitor's price. Further assume the buyer will use your product 250 times each year, and the life cycle of your product is four years. This means the cost-per-use difference is $1.00 or one-tenth of 1 percent (0.1 percent) every time the buyer uses it (4 years × 250 uses per year). Reducing the price difference and extending it over a four-year time period stretches the buyer's time horizon and poses a strong argument. Obsessing on a ridiculously small number is a waste of time for the buyer. For example: "Is a 0.1 percent difference, or $1.00, every time you use this product really that big of a deal when you consider the support we have given you and the value bundled into our solution?"

Fractionalizing is a way to present your price against a broader cost structure or backdrop. This is especially useful when your product represents a small part or a component of some bigger product or project. Assume you sell computer chips and these chips represent about 1 percent of the total cost of building a computer. Focus on the price difference between you and the competition. For example: "The difference between our solution and the competition's represents less than 1 percent of the total cost of the end product. Does it really make sense to make a decision based on pennies?"

In this example, fractionalizing the price difference shifts the buyer's focus onto the broader cost base. Assume the price differential between you and the competition is $1,000. Assume further this is for 1,000 pieces or components. This means the real cost difference is $1.00 per component. Assume each component is a small part of an item that costs $100 per unit to manufacture. The difference between you and the competition is 1 percent. That sounds much better than $1,000. If your component is a mission-critical part, does it really make sense for the buyer to introduce risk for 1 percent? Combining these strategies allows you to present a compelling argument.

Reverse the Objection

To reverse an objection, use the objection as the reason the buyer should reconsider her position. The momentum from her objection adds energy to your response. For example: "Ms. Buyer, if your real concern is money, that's exactly why I suggest you take another look at our proposal. The design of our solution is to help you achieve long-term operational efficiency and enjoy the cost savings as a result of implementing our solution."

Notice the word *money* is used, not price. Shifting the focus from price to money opens up a broader dialogue with the buyer over cost. There are several ways beyond price that you can affect the buyer's profitability. Elaborate on the value in your proposition. Discuss the impact or outcome of implementing your solution. When the buyer raises a money objection, she is giving you an opportunity to present a compelling counterargument. Here is another example: "The fact that you've raised money concerns is the very reason you must take another look at all the ways we have a positive financial impact on your business."

Again, you must elaborate on the positive financial outcome. This is a much better conversation to have with the buyer than an argument over the acquisition price. For salespeople, there is something personally gratifying in taking the buyer's objection and using it as the most compelling reason to buy.

Sell the Opportunity Value of Your Proposal

When your product or solution gives the buyer an opportunity to do something he has been unable to do in the past, use that as your cost justification. For example: "The advantage of working with us is that we give you the ability to do something tomorrow you cannot do today . . ."

One of my clients sells corrugated boxes. His packaging design helped his customer penetrate a retail chain they had tried unsuccessfully to penetrate for years. The prices for their corrugated boxes were 50 percent higher than the competition, but they got the business despite the higher price. The reason they got the business was that their packaging solution helped the buyer gain a new piece of business.

To build your response, ask yourself these questions:

- "What do we give the buyer the opportunity to pursue today that they could not pursue yesterday?"
- "What will they be able to do tomorrow that they cannot do today?"
- "What problems can they now solve that they could not have solved in the past?"

You can present this as the opportunity value in your solution. It is an incentive for the buyer to choose your solution.

The difference between price and cost is significant. Price is used mostly to exclude suppliers. If your price is higher, you are out of the competition. Getting the cheapest price sounds prudent and miserly at the same time. Shopping for the cheapest price introduces an element of risk that the solution may not work. When buyers perceive the opportunity value in your solution, they recognize that the risk of paying more than they anticipated is overshadowed by the potential opportunity gain.

Probe for Discretionary Funding

Companies shift money back and forth into different budget categories or accounts depending on their most pressing needs. Most of the sales training I conduct every year is funded from some other budget category such as advertising. Another way of viewing this is that few of my buyers have a budget for sales training. The need surfaces, they want to act on that need, and they find the money. The benefit of selling at the highest levels in an organization is that these people create budgets. Anyone who creates a budget can re-create a budget. One way to determine if the buyer has extra money is to ask this question, "Would you move forward if you had the money?" Pause. "It has been my experience in business when someone likes an idea, he can find discretionary funding. Is that the case here?"

You may discover the buyer likes and respects your candor. Dig for discretionary funding. The worst thing the buyer can tell you is that she does not have that flexibility. At least you have caused the buyer to consider alternatives. This idea works especially well when your solution helps the buyer increase his top line sales or swell his bottom line. Other budget categories may not offer that potential gain for the buyer, which makes your solution a better decision.

CHAPTER SUMMARY

Some buyers confuse price with cost. There are several driving forces behind the cost-based money objection, and buyers often misread the mandate they receive. You learned five ways to respond to cost-based money objections. Fundamental to your success in responding to these objections is stretching the buyer's time horizon so cost is spread out over the life cycle of your product. Your challenge moving forward is to educate the buyer to make a decision that takes into account the full scope of his or her needs.

15

Responding to Value-Based Money Objections

Price shoppers value-strip. They want your solution to meet the same criteria as your competition's so that they can reduce the decision to the cheapest price. If everyone meets the first-cut criteria, price rules the day. What if you could only compete on your differences and not price? How would your selling change?

This chapter is about dealing with the third type of money objections— value-based money objections. Value-based money objections come in two varieties. One, the buyer does not see the difference between you and the competition, and two, the buyer does not perceive the value in your proposition. Because there is so much to say about these, I could easily make the case for two separate chapters, but these two types of objections have a common root—a perception of value. You can change the buyer's mind and stand out from the crowd. You can prove your value to the buyer. The following information presented in this chapter will help you do just that:

- The two types of value-based money objections
- Twenty ways to respond to these objections

By studying these concepts and integrating them into your response strategy, you will be able to engage confidently and effectively value-based money objections.

DRIVING FORCES BEHIND VALUE-BASED MONEY OBJECTIONS

This type of money objection is different from price-based or cost-based money objections, covered in previous chapters. Price and cost objections presume the buyer has limited resources to work with. Value-based objections expose a different lack on the buyer's end—a lack of conviction about your solution. The buyer either fails to recognize the difference between your products or services and the competition or does not perceive the value in your proposition. Both of these objections are answerable. You can respond effectively if you maintain the correct focus of the objection: a perceived lack of value.

This perceived inequity is fundamental to the buyer's resistance. On one hand, the buyer perceives an inequitable relationship of your price vis-à-vis the competitor's price because of similarities in your packages. This inequity is more external because the comparison is made against another source. When the perceived inequity is your price vis-à-vis your package, this inequity is more internal because the comparison is made using only your value and your price. Internal and external refer to the reference point—the competition or you. In either case, you are dealing with the buyer's perception of the value you offer, so it is not really a price objection; it is a value-for-the-money objection. The buyer just does not see the value in your proposition. This is why you must be clear on your value proposition. It is the answer to the broad question, What do we do for you? Your presentation focuses on how you do it. The information that fills your presentation fuels your responses to value-based money objections.

LACK OF DIFFERENTIATION

The first type of value-based money objection is a perceived lack of differentiation. The buyer does not recognize or accept the differences between you and the competition. Our sales training experiences have confirmed studies that more than half of all salespeople fail to differentiate themselves from the competition. Is it any wonder buyers view things through a commodity prism?

It is in your DNA to be different. You have a genetic mandate to stand out. Your sales challenge and the purpose of this section is to convince the buyer that you are outstanding. When the buyer says, "You and so-and-so are all in the same business," your response must be, "We are in the same industry, but we are certainly not in the same business, and here's why." These eleven responses will help you stand out from the competition.

Cast Doubt

This works well with an existing customer since you have proven yourself repeatedly. You have a history of delivering value. You have earned the status and reputation of a trusted supplier. Couple that with the fact that 70 percent of your customers are low-risk individuals, and you have an effective way to respond to a price objection: "We know what it is going to cost you to pay a bit more to go with our guaranteed package of value. The only unknown variable at this point is, what are you accustomed to getting from us today that you risk losing tomorrow?"

This is another way of asking the customer: "What's a good night's sleep worth to you? The advantage of our solution is that we take care of the things that might cause you to stay awake at night if you went with an unproven alternative."

You can sell against the competition without bad-mouthing them. Distance yourself with a proven track record against a competitor's promise to do what you are already doing. If you have a proven track record, you should not have to match any interlopers' prices. They should improve to compete with you. Performance trumps promises every time.

Tap Into Security Needs

When your product is a vital part of the buyer's application, can he really afford to go with a cheap alternative? Raise this issue with the following question: "Is price the safest decision you can make at this point?" Emphasize the word *safest* in this question. It jumps out at the buyer. *Safest* is emotionally packed. It refocuses the buyer on the critical issue, which is not price.

If you sell a smaller component of a much bigger item, price is less of an issue. For example, if you sell a mission-critical part to a manufacturer, can the buyer really afford to go cheap for this? Your product is too critical to price shop. Refocus the buyer with this question: "When you look at the critical nature of this part, is this really where you want to save a few pennies? Do you really want to introduce that element of risk to this project?"

These questions point out that a decision to buy cheaper introduces unnecessary risk. Few buyers will go out of their way to introduce risk to their decision. You are safe. You are proven. Tell the buyer that he never has to apologize for the security you provide.

Point Out the Risk of Cheapness

Paying a little more than what a buyer anticipates pales by comparison to not getting what he needs, when he needs it, to do the job he wants to do. Raising this issue with the buyer in the form of a question calls attention to that possibility. This is especially effective when your product represents a small part of a bigger purchase he is making. This question exposes the greater risk of receiving less when purchasing the cheaper alternative: "In your opinion, and considering your objectives, which offers you a greater risk at this point: paying a little more than you anticipated on the front end or not getting what you need on the back end to achieve the results that you are looking for?"

This question is a thought provoker because the seller is comparing paying a little more than the buyer anticipated with the potential of not getting the strongest benefit the seller offers. Weighing your advantage against paying more than he anticipated is fair game. This helps the buyer focus on critical decision variables other than price. It could be quality parts, readily available inventory, vital technical support, or the real nightmare scenario of not meeting his timeline for the project. Which do you think scares the buyer more, paying more than he anticipated or not completing a major project on time?

Consider the Bottom-Line Impact

There are countless examples in business of people who have attempted to save money on the front end only to have it absorbed by overhead on the back end. For example, a cheaper product that does not include assembly costs the buyer assembly time. If the buyer does not value his time, your challenge is to help him understand that assembling a product may not be the best use of his time. Is this a case in which the buyer is being penny-wise and pound-foolish? You may say, "I understand there is a difference in our pricing, but will that difference in pricing really show up on your bottom line, or is it conceivable it will be absorbed by overhead before it ever hits your bottom line?"

Sometimes, a front-end savings is meaningless by the time it reaches the buyer's bottom line. Maybe your competition offers a phony savings on the front end because the operating costs are higher during ownership. If a competitor's product is cheaper to buy but more costly to operate, it has a negative impact on the buyer's bottom line.

On the other hand, if your product costs more to purchase but less to operate over the long haul, your product is a better long-term business decision. You can illustrate this difference and reassure the buyer by creating a value analysis that demonstrates the total cost of ownership and usage. Include enough input variables as necessary to demonstrate the hidden costs of ownership and usage with the competition's package. The fundamental strategy here should look familiar. You are stretching the time horizon to promote ownership and value, not just acquisition price.

Throw the Competitive Boomerang

The buyer sometimes uses a competitor's price to intimidate you: "I can buy this cheaper from another source" or "Your competition offered us a better deal." Use the momentum of the objection to redirect the conversation back to the buyer. You can defend your price without getting defensive. Remain on the offensive. Ask the buyer why he thinks the competition is cheaper: "Do you know why they are cheaper? If they say they are cheaper, I cannot argue their case for them. I really cannot justify their decision to sell at a lower price. They are in a much better position than I am to comment on the value of what they are selling. I can only explain the value we bring. If they say they are worth less, I would take their word for it."

With this response you are saying, "We are not defensive about our price, but I would be concerned why the competition is charging so little." Staying on the offensive projects confidence. There is no need to defend what need not be defended. This response is verbal judo. It is defending without being defensive. For some buyers, your lack of taking the bait shocks them into realizing the competition is cheaper for a reason. Do they want to experience that cheapness firsthand?

The Alternate Advantage Overload

Acknowledge the higher price and use it as a backdrop to reiterate your other competitive advantages. Acknowledging this higher price gives you positive momentum. For example: "Sure, we're higher on price. The reason we're higher on price is that we're higher in every other critical area as well. You can't be high in those areas and low in price; it doesn't work that way in business. I know it doesn't work that way in your business."

Notice the strategy of invoking empathy here by saying it does not work that way in *your* business. You are appealing to the buyer's sense of fairness. This is covered in depth later in this chapter. Acknowledging, not apologizing for, this higher price is one more opportunity to brag about the value your company delivers and the value for which the buyer expressed a preference.

Focus on the Difference, Not the Savings

When there is a price difference between you and the competition, expunge the word *savings* from your vocabulary. Replace it with the word *difference*. You can acknowledge the difference in price and use it to launch your value-added presentation. "Sure, there is a difference in our price. I would be shocked if there weren't. The reason there is a small difference in our price is there is a huge difference in what we bring you. Let's review all the things that make us different."

This is precisely the point at which you want to use a value analysis that favors your solution. You want to minimize the difference in price and maximize the difference of the value in your package.

Stake Out Your Mainstream Position

Some people believe when they request bids, they can throw out the top and bottom bids and select the middle bid to get what they need at a reasonable price. You can tap into this mainstream supplier thinking by saying: "Sure, our prices are higher than some suppliers, and we are also lower than other suppliers. If you look around, you will find others who charge more than we do and others who charge less than we do. One of the things we are most confident of is that our pricing is as mainstream as it gets."

Emphasize *mainstream*. There is an attitude in business-to-business selling that no one ever got fired for choosing a mainstream solution. It is safe; it is proven; and it has a positive reputation. This is the position you want to own in the buyer's mind. It reassures people to know they have chosen a mainstream solution. This buyer is in a psychological comfort zone when he thinks, "I did not pay too much or too little." Depending on your relationship and history with the customer, you can use this response: "We're not the cheapest and we're not the most expensive, but we're the one you're talking to about this because we've earned the right with our performance not to be the cheapest or have to compete just on price." Or you can try this one: "I am surprised at your reaction. We really study this issue and are confident we are priced in the mainstream."

The implication in all these responses is that the competition may be out of the mainstream. You want to be the benchmark by which everyone else is judged.

Present a "Ten Things to Consider" List

Ten degrees of separation or differentiation between you and the competition makes the buying decision easier. Ten compelling differences justify a single difference in price. Say to the buyer: "Many people ask us why they should choose us over a competitor. To help with that decision process, we have prepared a decision-making tool for you. Notice the heading for this tool is 'Ten Reasons to Consider Our Solution Over the Competition.' This means you can choose any competitor, and we still deliver value in these ten areas."

This response effectively genericizes the competition. You did not target a specific competitor. You said, "It does not matter to whom you compare us, here are ten reasons why you should choose us." This reduces every other supplier to a commodity and positions your solution as the value-added solution. Your confidence and enthusiasm are contagious. Pride and passion work well together. Being proud of your differences and presenting them with passion reassures the buyer he is making the right decision.

Acknowledge Generic Similarities

Every product meets a core-commodity need. Buyers commoditize suppliers and products when they compare only generic similarities. You counter this with a conversation about everything that makes you stand out. You can say to the buyer, "The only similarity between us and the competition is that we are in the same industry. How we approach your needs is as unique as your needs. We never treat our customers as if they have generic needs. Here's how our customers say we're special."

At this point, elaborate on your differences. Explain how you deliver value. Demonstrate how you stand out in the industry. Another way to respond is: "For us to accept your premise that all suppliers are the same negates what makes us special. The value of our relationships with customers is not determined by the price we charge but the impact we have on their businesses. Isn't that what you ultimately buy—results?"

Spreadsheet the Decision

A spreadsheet decision is a value analysis. The spreadsheet includes all variables that affect cost. Begin with a list of decision input variables and weigh them accordingly. You may weight variables differently, depending on the buyer's priorities: purchase price, installation costs, training, packaging options, service intervals, trade-in value, residual value, etc. On the spreadsheet, detail how your decision makes sense for the buyer vis-à-vis the competition. Some purchasing agents perform this value analysis on their own. For buyers, the spreadsheet is quantitative proof of your argument—the justification they need to give you the order. Prepare in advance. Having it in hand allows you to stay on the sales offensive.

THE BUYER DOES NOT PERCEIVE YOUR VALUE

When the buyer does not perceive or appreciate your value, you must reiterate everything you do for the customer. Review the full scope and impact of your value. This response strategy is really educating the buyer. You may notice a pattern with these responses. You are fighting a battle over the focal point of the conversation. It will either center on the price of something or on the value of that solution—what it is ultimately worth to the buyer. Your resolve, coupled with a strong argument, are just the right weapons to help you win this battle. Here are nine ways to do that.

Cash in Your Chips

In the same way most people are unaware of the air they breathe, most customers are unaware of the value they receive. At one time, they may have known and appreciated all the special things you did for them, but customers' memories are short. When you cash in your chips, remind customers of the things you do for them within the context of how the customer has benefited. It is not bragging about your service; it is celebrating the impact your value has on the customer. For example, you may say, "Look at our history over the past few years. You know what to expect from us. Is it worth giving up that security and peace of mind for a small price differential?"

No one gets the credit they deserve; they only get the credit they ask for. Cashing in your chips is your way of getting the credit you deserve for the value you contribute to the customer's business. You owe it to yourself and your company to get recognition for this value.

Trial Close

The trial close isolates price as the only reason the buyer is hesitating and contrasts it to broader agreement for choosing your solution. Ask two questions:

- "Ms. Buyer, if you were to make a decision today on any and all variables other than price, who would you go with and why?" (Pause and wait for the buyer to respond. Assume the buyer offers four reasons why she wants to work with you.)
- "Doesn't it make more sense to go with us and get four out of the five things you are looking for than to go with the competition and get only one of the five, which is simply a cheaper price?"

In this example, you ask the buyer to contrast all the reasons she wants to do business with you versus the competition's cheaper price. She gives you four reasons why she likes your offer and only one reason she leans toward the competition. Your response focuses on these four reasons. The buyer hands you the most compelling reasons why price should not be an issue. You are delivering four important things she needs, and the competition is tempting her with only a cheaper price.

Reinforce Your Uniqueness

Reinforcing uniqueness is another opportunity to brag about your solution. It demonstrates pride and self-confidence. Only someone who genuinely believes in his company and product can say, "We made a decision a long time ago that it is easier for us to justify our price one time than to repeatedly apologize for a lack of quality or service."

Tell the buyer you made a choice to compete on everything you do for him, not just price. Shift the focus off price and onto everything you do. There is no apology for high quality or great service. Explain your quality and service without apologizing for your price. You are unique and do not want the buyer to trivialize this uniqueness.

Invoke Empathy

In Chapter 10, I demonstrated how expressing empathy acknowledges your understanding of the buyer's concerns without validating the objection. In this example, the buffer expresses empathy without agreeing that price should drive the decision. For example, "Ms. Buyer, I understand price is one part of your overall profitability analysis."

Invoking empathy draws the buyer in to your point of view by asking her to consider your position. This means tying your response to something with which the buyer can identify. For example: "Like you, we made a decision a long time ago that we could compete successfully in our market based on the quality of our product and service, not just on price. We lose a few opportunities each year because of this, but we gain more than we lose. We hope that's the case here."

Invoke empathy with the first two words, "like you." This makes it relevant and personal for the buyer. If the buyer loses business because of price, your statement resonates with her. Empathizing with you is the first step to her understanding and accepting your argument.

Another example is invoking the feeling the buyer has about her price competitor. Transfer these feelings to your number one price competitor. If Brand X is your price competition and Brand Z is her price competition, your response sounds like this: "I understand your request for a cheaper price. The problem we are dealing with is our competitor, Brand X, is really the Brand Z of our industry. Like you, we must deal with price competitors who really only offer a cheaper price."

You are hoping the buyer will transfer her negative feelings for her price competitor to your price competitor. Be careful with this response. You must know your buyer well and enjoy some rapport to invoke her price competitor's name in your response.

Ask the Bandwagon Question

Reassurance comes in different forms. The bandwagon question paves the way for your demonstrating support from other customers. This strategy is effective for two reasons. First, buyers want to know others have enjoyed success with your product. It reassures them. Second, during periods of uncertainty, people gravitate to the herd. There is safety in numbers. Knowing others approve of your product provides comfort, cover, and justification. "Mr. Buyer, many of the people we work with today have asked us why they should pay more to do business with us. Would you like to read what they have said?"

At this point, produce testimonial letters or endorsements from other customers. Have this information at your fingertips for the buyer to study. If your buyer must justify this decision to a higher authority, you are giving him the proof that he needs to argue your case.

Offer a Performance Contract

This strategy works well in some industries. There may be a seed of an idea in this strategy for your application. The buyer and seller write performance standards into the proposal, and the seller earns a bonus for achieving these standards. This happens often in the construction industry. If you complete a project on time and under budget, you share in the savings. For example: "We are willing to revisit this in six months to ensure we have performed to specs. If we have not achieved what we promise you today with these objective buying criteria, we forfeit any performance incentives. We absorb a major part of the risk for the timely completion of this project."

Some contracts also have a clause for a failure to perform called a *malus*. The seller must repay or forfeit some money to the buyer for failing to perform. The fundamental dynamic with this response strategy is that you lower risk for the buyer by earning a bonus or forfeiting payment. The more risk you assume, the less resistance you face to your prices. Buyers find security in your willingness to absorb risk. If the performance contract is not viable in this form, ask yourself how you can minimize the risk for your buyers, "What can we do to share or reduce risk for our buyers?"

Reassure the Buyer

The guarantee or warranty is similar to the performance contract. They all reduce or share risk. Be sure to stress the positive applications of your warranty versus the remedies. Guarantee the buyer's complete satisfaction with your solution. For example: "Ms. Buyer, we recognize that a guarantee or warranty may sound like a remedy. We like to emphasize the more positive aspects of our guarantee—to work with you until you are completely satisfied. We are guaranteeing your complete satisfaction with our solution."

Do you think the buyer wants you to give her money back? No. Why would she want to waste her time and resources on that type of remedy? The buyer wants reassurance she is going to get exactly what she needs, and your guarantee sets a positive tone for the buyer. You are reassuring her you will perform until she is completely satisfied with your solution. Where is the risk here?

A different application of this concept is the extended warranty. Some companies use extended warranties as a profit center. What if you presented it as a differentiator? This means you automatically extend for free the warranty for what you sell. It demonstrates your faith in your products and helps you stand out from the competition. Some people may bristle at the thought of just giving this away. If your products are good and buyers use them responsibly, where's the risk? The profit you make on holding firm on prices can offset the extended warranty revenue. You earn it on the front end or the back end.

Offer a Personal Guarantee

Few salespeople take advantage of this powerful way to combat price objections. If you have earned credibility with a customer, you have earned the right to say, "Mr. Buyer, I have been in this territory for fifteen years and plan to be here another fifteen years. I am not going to squander a thirty-year career in my territory for an order. If we fail to perform as I have promised here today, this is something that will affect me personally as well. That is how confident I am of our solution."

If you have earned the buyer's trust because of your performance in your territory, most people understand you will not squander this goodwill for an order. Laying it all on the line is a persuasive argument. Who can doubt your sincerity or confidence when you are willing to go all-out for this order?

Use the VIP List, Three Questions, and Walk

In our section on preparation, I discussed the importance of having a list of your value added, in the form of a value-in-purchasing list. This is a valuable tool to use when the buyer gives you a price objection. For example: "Mr. Buyer, I have a suggestion. Before you make your final decision, I ask you to review our proposal one more time. Toward the back of the proposal you will see our VIP list. It is our value-in-purchasing list. Please study this. Once you have done that, ask yourself these three questions about the competitive options you are considering."

Pose three questions to spotlight the differences in your proposal vis-à-vis competitors—areas where you are uniquely strong. This could include questions about your unique selling proposition. Be prepared with these questions. Know them in advance. Your success with this strategy requires preparation. Next, you must know your walking point and be prepared to walk. The buyer must witness your steely resolve.

CHAPTER SUMMARY

Some buyers fail to perceive your value. Their objections appear as either equity or value-based objections. In the first type, the buyer perceives no difference between you and the competition. This is a lack of differentiation. In the second, the buyer fails to see the value in your proposition. Your overall strategy is to reiterate your value and uniqueness. Specifically, you learned twenty ways to respond to value-based money objections. You can remain steady in these selling situations where the buyer simply needs more information about what makes you special. This means you must be ready to answer these two questions: "What are your definable and defendable differences?" and "Where is the value in your proposition?" Your challenge will be to keep the focus of the conversation on the value you provide versus the price the buyer wants to pay.

16

Responding to Game-Based Money Objections

My father said: "You must never try to make all the money that's in a deal. Let the other fellow make some money too, because if you have a reputation for always making all the money there is in a deal, you won't make many deals."

—J. PAUL GETTY, AMERICAN INDUSTRIALIST

This is the essence of win-win negotiating. Unfortunately, not everyone subscribes to this philosophy. Some buyers wield any advantage to drive down their suppliers' prices. These tactics come at a heavy price—a strained relationship with their supply partners. Salespeople who lack negotiating savvy fall prey to these buyers' games.

This chapter is about dealing with the fourth type of money objection—negotiating games. Game-based money objections involve gambits and maneuvers designed to achieve a desired outcome. Here are the key points covered in this chapter:

- The win-win negotiating philosophy
- Five rules for negotiating win-win outcomes
- Twelve tips to become a more effective negotiator

By studying these concepts and integrating them into your response strategy, you will be able to negotiate desirable and equitable outcomes from a position of strength and knowledge, dealing successfully with game-based money objections.

WIN-WIN NEGOTIATING PHILOSOPHY

Equity has been a major theme throughout this book. It always bears repeating that people must feel they get as good as they give. This perception of equity is fundamental to positive energy in a negotiation. It is difficult to look out for someone else when you feel no one is looking out for you. Negotiations have ended unsuccessfully because one or both parties felt the exchange was too one-sided. There are only two possible negotiating outcomes: win-win and lose-lose.

An "I win, and you lose" outcome means you, as the buyer, accept my offer but resent it and find another supplier as soon as possible. I ultimately lose. An "I lose, and you win" outcome means I accept the order but bristle at what I gave up to get it. Because of this perceived inequity, I resent the business, and my service likely suffers. You ultimately lose. We both lose.

"Lose-lose" outcomes describe an end result where both parties make enough concessions that there appears to be no winners, only losers. Some negotiators define this latter option as the best possible outcome because there are no "individual winners." I find a double-loss outcome a poor definition of winning. It follows then that we either both win or both lose.

The win-win philosophy begins with a simple objective: we both must benefit from the outcome of the negotiation, which means it is a good deal for both of us. When you begin with a win-win objective, the games, gambits, and maneuvers are unnecessary, because your strategy is to work cooperatively to achieve the results you both want and need. Laying out this desired outcome early in the negotiation sets a positive tone for the rest of the exchange: "Mr. Buyer, I appreciate the opportunity to work with you on this project and to achieve the win-win outcome we both need and want."

What happens when the buyer ignores your positive intent and chooses to play games? You cannot control the outcome of these situations. You can control only what you put into them. Remind yourself of your commitment to a win-win outcome and reassert your position to the buyer. This presumes you are dealing with reasonable buyers. If not, it is a different selling problem: targeting the wrong business.

NEGOTIATING RULES

Even though you have planned for a win-win outcome, things do not always go your way. Despite your best intentions, the buyer's self-interests may overwhelm the spirit of cooperation you have created. These four rules will help steady your response when faced with negotiating games.

Rule #1: Watch Your Energy

Fear is the wrong energy to bring to a negotiation. John F. Kennedy warned against this in his inaugural address: "Let us never negotiate out of fear, but let us never fear to negotiate." If you negotiate out of fear, you operate from a defensive position of guarding and protecting your turf. Your focus is directed solely at your position. You are negotiating not to lose.

If you negotiate from a position of hope and optimism, you are on the offensive. You are creating a desirable outcome versus defending a position. The outcome you are creating is win-win. You are negotiating *for* something, not *against* something. You are negotiating for equity, not just self-interests. This attitude is contagious. Once the buyer realizes your intent, he can relax his defenses and seek the common ground for the common good.

Rule #2: Spot the Game

See it and accept it for what it is. Your recognition of the game strips it of its power. You know the buyer is playing a role. You are choosing not to participate in the game. Volumes are written on the types of games buyers play. Knowing how to spot them ensures you do not get duped into playing them. Common games include the following:

▪ **Stiff-arm.** The buyer issues an ultimatum: "This is my final offer." "Take it or leave it." "It's my way or the highway." If you have ever been on the receiving end of this, you know that buyers change their minds. Within a few minutes, the buyer may reconsider once he sees you are not responding to the game.

▪ **Feigning ignorance.** The buyer makes statements or asks questions that cause you to question his ability to make a good decision. Be careful. Some buyers are dumb like a fox. Anytime you are confronted with a buyer who appears uncharacteristically dumb, be aware it could be a game to draw you into a false sense of security. Then, when you are most vulnerable, the buyer makes his request.

■ **The shocker.** This is any outrageous request or act designed to get you off your game. Emotionalism is an example of this. Asking for unreasonable concessions is another. The logic follows that if the buyer does something or asks for something to shock you, you will be relieved when he settles down and makes a reasonable request for a smaller concession.

■ **The carrot.** In this game, the buyer holds in front of you the promise of future business. When buyers dangle the carrot, it is because they know what they are feeding you now will leave you hungry. Focus on the immediate opportunity, knowing if you perform beyond his expectations, the future business will happen. Do not fall for this promise of future business. If you relent on price now, you will need to discount again in the future.

■ **The competitive stooge.** The buyer tells you that the competition has offered an incredible price—too good to pass up. If that is true, why is the buyer still talking to you? For some reason, the other deal is not as sweet as the buyer makes it out to be. You must be thinking, *If the deal were that good, why didn't the buyer go for it?* You may even want to ask the question, "Mr. Buyer, there are obviously some reasons you still want to work with us; would you share those with me?"

Buyers use other games, too. These examples encourage you to spot gambits or maneuvers designed to drive down prices. See the game for what it is—a ploy.

Rule #3: Choose Not to Play

Resist participating in games. Your refusal to play signals your recognition of the game. Refusing to play is maintaining control of the conversation. This decision boosts your self-confidence because you decide your next move. When you refuse to play the game, the buyer has little choice but to return to the negotiation.

Refusing to play reminds you of your win-win objective. Refocus your energy on identifying an equitable solution; this will prevent you from getting defensive. Once you get defensive, you have chosen to participate in the games.

Rule #4: Acknowledge the Game and Seek Resolution

Acknowledging the buyer's tactic demonstrates your sensitivity to the process, and finessing your response dismisses the game. For example, if there is heightened emotion in the game or selling scenario, you can diffuse the emotion by saying, "I know there is a lot of emotion in this decision. My hope is that it does not blind us to a great resolution."

Your use of the word *us* assumes some ownership for the emotion. The buyer feels no need to defend it. Acknowledging, not agreeing with, the game tells the buyer this is not your first negotiation. For a buyer who throws up roadblocks like the stiff-arm, you can say, "How can we solve this if one of us is going to shut down the process?"

Rule #5: Respond with a Win-Win Attitude

If your attitude is win-win and you do not get distracted by the negotiating noise and gamesmanship, you will maintain your positive focus. Your attitude and response to all games must be, "I know there is a good deal in here for both of us if we are willing to hang in there long enough to find it." Your persistent and positive focus will redirect the conversation down a double-win path.

NEGOTIATING TIPS

Negotiating is using whatever power and influence is at one's disposal to achieve a desired outcome. It is conferring with others to find common ground for agreement. Parents negotiate with children on curfews and car privileges. Managers negotiate salaries, time off, and assignments with employees. Husbands and wives negotiate over weekend plans and chores. Friends negotiate over entertainment options. Negotiating is all around us. We do it daily, though we are underprepared for it. This section will help prepare you for this inevitable practice.

Tip #1: Prepare Like Your Future Depends on It, Because It Does

Preparation is a critical factor in a successful negotiation. Whoever is better prepared for price negotiations—you or the buyer—has a better chance of achieving the desired outcome. Planning and preparation lower risk. In a 2007 study, the Strategic Account Management Association and Think, Inc., reported 83 percent of strategic account managers had no negotiating strategy. These are high-level salespeople. You would think they would know better.

Prepare for the negotiation by understanding what you must have and what you would like to have. Do the same for the buyer—study his needs and wants. Visualize the win-win outcome you desire. What trade-offs are you prepared to make? How much pressure is the buyer feeling to do business with you?

The time to answer these questions is before you sit down at the negotiating table.

Tip #2: *Never* Rarely Means *Never*

Buyers who stiff-arm and say, "This is my final deal," may not mean it. How many times have you heard someone say that and minutes later change her mind? The easiest way to engineer a different outcome is to give the buyer an opportunity to save face. Offer a different decision to draw the buyer back into the process. Give the buyer a reason to say yes.

Tip #3: Buyers Always Speak on the Record

There is never a time when buyers are off-the-record. For example, if you and a customer are at a ball game and the customer says, "Off the record, how's business?" anything you say in response to that question is on the tape inside the buyer's head, and she will use it in future negotiations. If you tell the buyer your business is faltering, it is a good time for her to ask for a price concession. Be cautious with your response. Buyers and sellers should maintain enough professional distance in their personal relationships to make the tough calls and difficult decisions.

Tip #4: Whoever Feels the Most Pressure Makes the Most Concessions

Most concessions are made toward the end of a negotiation, not at the beginning. This is why professional negotiators hold their most important issue for the end of the discussion. They want to capitalize on the negotiating momentum by using the other person's desire to end the negotiation. The critical dynamic at work here is timing. In sales, timing is everything. Follow the words of the great American musician, Kenny Rogers: "You got to know when to hold 'em. Know when to fold 'em." If you understand how to use time in a negotiation, you can maintain your win-win focus.

Tip #5: Trade Concessions

When it comes to concessions, the rule of thumb is to trade concessions, not make concessions. Be selective with and protective of your concessions. One study found 79 percent of salespeople occasionally trade for buyer demands. In most cases, salespeople give away their value. One successful sales manager taught his sales force to give away nothing without asking for something in return. He called it the tit-for-tat principle: "I'll do this if you'll do that." Otherwise, buyers will think there is an endless parade of concessions you can make. When you ask for a concession in return, the buyer realizes the give-and-take dynamic of his request and your response.

Tip #6: Get Your Ego out of It

When negotiating price, do not let your ego get in the way. You cannot deal with someone else's ego when your own is out of control. If you identify with your company and believe in your product, your emotional attachment is a burden and a blessing. It is a blessing when it emerges as passion. It is a burden when it expresses defensiveness. Which is more important to you, looking good in negotiating or negotiating good deals for your company? Treat the other person with respect and enjoy the benefits of reciprocity. You get back what you give to others.

Tip #7: Slow Down the Process

Prudently drag your feet. When negotiating price, time and emotion are your two biggest enemies. Prudently drag your feet to slow down the process. Give yourself time and space to make good decisions. Conceding and agreeing under pressure guarantees seller remorse after the negotiation. How many decisions have you made that might have turned out differently had you slept on them? Have you ever said either of the following to yourself: "Gee, I wish I hadn't said that." "Boy, I wish I had said that."?

Tip #8: Aim High, Go Low

Some salespeople believe you must lead with a higher price to leave yourself negotiating room. Their strategy is to aim high and go low. Professional negotiators call this a *hold-back position*. They hold something in reserve for last-minute incentives. There are pro and con arguments to be made for this approach. On the one hand, this is a game, which we are trying to avoid in win-win negotiating. On the other hand, some buyers need a win. Your call.

Tip #9: Use Funny Money

Funny money includes delivery time, delivery charges, follow-up support, technical assistance, installation, training, terms, additional goods, special packaging, extended warranty, consulting time, or maybe rebates for frequent buying. If you use funny money versus real money, you gain negotiating leverage. Your cost of funny money is much lower than cash, but the perceived value for the buyer remains high. For example, your cost of offering consulting services is the value of your time. If you have more time than money, your cost is low. The value of your consulting services to the customer is high because your focus is to have an impact on his business. Bundling this service into your total solution increases its perceived value without increasing the price.

Tip #10: Flinch at the First Offer

Flinching is reacting visibly when a buyer makes you an offer or requests a concession. Otherwise, you arouse her suspicions, and the buyer thinks she did not ask for enough. Flinching may include a look of surprise on your face, an innocent comment reflecting your surprise, or any other nonverbal signal that indicates you cannot accept the request. You are trying to be convincing here, you are not competing for an Oscar. Too much drama is transparent. Take time to consider the offer or request. Is it a good business decision? What can you ask for in return?

This raises another issue. Silence is useful in negotiating to nudge the process along. A pregnant pause inserted opportunistically in a conversation can move the buyer. Some people believe that whoever blinks first loses. This attitude reflects a win-lose approach. Offering a new decision for the other person to save face is not conceding; it is cooperating. It is engineering an equitable outcome both parties can embrace.

Tip #11: Do Not Split First

Whoever makes the opening move for concessions goes more than halfway in meeting the other person's request. Beware and be aware of what you offer. It may result in a win-lose outcome. Your offer to split the difference means the final result will be closer to the buyer's position than your position. For example, if your price is $10,000 and the buyer wants to pay $9,000, do not offer to split the difference. It sounds cooperative, but the buyer will likely say, "That's still more than I wanted to pay." This means you will settle for a price closer to $9,000 than $10,000. Let the other person suggest the split. You may need to solicit this by asking, "What can we do at this point to find some common ground?" Let the buyer respond by taking the initiative to split first. This applies to any concession, including money, time, delivery, terms, etc. This will help you settle closer to your desired outcome.

Tip #12: Agree to Disagree

When all else fails in a negotiation, you can agree to disagree and end things on a positive note. I have mentioned your walking point before. You must know when it is time to leave and have the courage to walk away from a bad deal. True negotiating power comes from knowing your limits. It is important to know what you can do. It is incredibly liberating to know what you cannot do. Let the buyer feel the full impact of his decisions to go cheap. He may return and be more receptive to your price. It is important to end on a positive note. Knowing how to lose is as important as knowing how to win. Everyone loves a good sport and resents a poor loser. Thank the buyer for his time and consideration.

CHAPTER SUMMARY

In responding to game-based money objections, it always best to strive to negotiate win-win outcomes for you and the buyer. Some buyers wield tactics and maneuvers to drive down your price. You have a choice to participate in these games. In this chapter, you learned five negotiating rules and twelve tips to become a better negotiator. You can maintain your negotiating integrity when others press you to make bad decisions. You can maintain your profitability by becoming a more knowledgeable and skilled negotiator. If you begin the negotiation with a win-win attitude and maintain it throughout the process, you will find most of the games you encounter will have little effect on the negotiation. You can sell more profitably if you become a more skilled negotiator.

17

Responding to Procedural-Based Money Objections

Rules are mostly made to be broken and are too often for the lazy to hide behind.

—GENERAL DOUGLAS MACARTHUR

This sounds like a variation of "There are rules, and then there are rules." One gets the impression that rules are fleeting, at the mercy of someone else's fancy. They provide sanctuary for bureaucrats and discouragement for the faint of heart. Some people hide behind rules, and others challenge them. A buyer who wants to dismiss a salesperson can easily hide behind a purchasing directive. For those in government procurement, policy may tie their hands. Salespeople who call on these buyers may let their frustrations end their pursuit before they explore all avenues.

This chapter is about dealing with the fifth type of money objection: procedural-based money objections. Of the five types of money objections, these may be the most difficult to resolve. Here are the topics covered in this chapter:

- Four ways to respond to procedural-based money objections
- Additional thoughts on dealing with price resistance

By studying these concepts and integrating them into your response strategy, you will be able to persist when the buying process seems to keep you out of it.

FORCES THAT DRIVE PROCEDURAL-BASED MONEY OBJECTIONS

This objection rears its head in several scenarios. First, you may be calling on a large account that has contract pricing with several major suppliers. This contract is a license to sell or to be part of the process without any guarantees of volume. Second, you may be calling on a government agency or municipality that is required by code or law to seek bids from different sources or purchase from contract-approved suppliers. Third, you may be calling on a purchasing agent who has told you her company has an internal approval process you must go through before you can sell.

First things first. Is this a real objection, or is the buyer stalling? I invited a director of purchasing to speak to a group of salespeople in one of my public seminars. He confessed to the group that one of the easiest ways to get rid of a salesperson is to request a quote on something. He said most salespeople leave the office thrilled to have the opportunity to spend time quoting a piece of business they probably will not get. It sounds cynical, but it is real.

Is the buyer hiding behind a policy because he does not want to tell you no directly? Is the buyer hiding behind a policy because he does not want to put in the extra effort to approve another supplier? Do not accept this objection at face value without digging deeper.

FOUR WAYS TO RESPOND

You want to stay in the fight as long as possible. You are in it until you or the buyer stops the process. Unless the buyer has specifically told you to stop, you are still in the game. Here are four things you can do to keep the ball rolling.

■ **Join the process.** Is it possible for you to participate in the bidding procedure? Can you help reshape the bidding process in a way to benefit you? Can you help the buyer write specifications? What would it take for you to become a preferred supplier? You must ask and answer these questions to design your response strategy.

■ **Offer contract pricing.** Offer your own contract to the buyer. What can you put in writing to satisfy the buyer's need for a contract? How have you done this with other customers? What are the buyer's criteria for a contract?

■ **Probe deeper.** Ask the buyer these two questions: "Do you ever have the occasion to buy off contract?" and "What do you do when you need something in an emergency?" You want the buyer to admit that she has bought off contract in the past. If she acknowledges that she has done this, it cracks open the door for your selling. You may find you will earn your way into the account one small emergency order at a time.

■ **Ask for a negotiated agreement.** A design-build construction firm wanted more negotiated contracts than bid business. Negotiated business was more profitable. They enjoyed success by asking the question: "What do you hope to accomplish with a bid you cannot get negotiating with us one-on-one?" They succeeded because they changed the conversation and the buyer's thinking. Prior to this question, the buyer thought the only way to secure the best deal was to put it out for bid. This firm reassured the buyer they could meet his needs equitably. It saved critical time, and the buyer got what he wanted—a double win.

ADDITIONAL THOUGHTS FOR PRICE OBJECTIONS

To review, we have traveled quite a distance in the past five chapters. You have learned how to respond to each of the five main types of money objections. We finish this part of the book with three additional thoughts for dealing with money objections. You can add these to your arsenal to increase your effectiveness.

Tip #1: Offer the Buyer a New Decision to Make

When the buyer says no, he feels the need to defend his position. You want to eliminate this defensiveness. Give him something to which he can say yes. Show him a different package that enables you to present a different price: "I have a different option for you to consider." If you make a price adjustment, emphasize that you have adjusted the price because you adjusted the package. The price adjustment is a result of changing the package. This maintains your credibility throughout the entire negotiation.

Tip #2: Help Your Buyer Save Face

Consider the psychology of dealing with objections. The buyer says no to you and your price. If you decide you are not going to change your price, you must say no to the buyer. This is a double rejection. For you to do business, someone must concede. For the buyer to reverse herself and go with your price, she may lose face. A buyer may want to change her mind but needs a way to save face in the process. Look for ways to help her save face. By applying Tip #1, giving the buyer a different decision to make, she saves face. Assuming some responsibility yourself for the stalemate also lets the buyer save face: "Maybe I can research some additional options for you and return with another idea."

Tip #3: Be More Gracious in Defeat than in Victory

Salespeople react differently to losing an order for which they have worked hard. On the one hand, they feel frustrated and angry. That is understandable. On the other hand, they can wish the buyer well and move on. Being gracious in defeat is a good strategy. Carrying around bitterness after you lose a sale is bad for your psyche. It is terrible for your positive attitude. Being gracious in defeat could mean sending your buyer a letter like the example shown here.

Consider the impact of this letter on the buyer when he receives it. You lost the business, yet you are incredibly gracious. You tell the buyer that you want to be his safety net. Do you think the door is wide open for the next opportunity? You bet it is. It is as important to know how to lose a piece of business as it is to win it.

"More Gracious in Defeat" Letter

Dear Mr. Buyer:

Thanks for the opportunity to work with you on this project. You have a lot of exciting initiatives going on in your company right now, and it was fun to be a part of the process. I understand you have made a decision to move in another direction. I respect this decision and know there will be other opportunities for us work together in the future.

Again, good luck on this project. If for some reason the other alternative does not work out, I want to be your go-to guy. Let us be your safety net on this project.

Sincerely,
Tom Reilly

CHAPTER SUMMARY

A procedural objection occurs when the buyer resists because a policy mandate restricts purchasing. It may be a national contract or law, in the case of government procurement, that mandates their options. This situation is not hopeless. You want to determine if it is real or a stall and seek to become part of the process or negotiate an arrangement that is mutually beneficial. Remember, you are still in the game until you or the buyer calls it quits. If you lose the business, be more gracious in defeat than in victory.

■ PART IV ■

LAGNIAPPE

Lagniappe: A Creole (Cajun) word to describe a little something extra.

Everyone likes a little something extra. Buy a dozen dough-nuts, and the baker throws in number thirteen for free. It is called a baker's dozen. Go to a candy shop and after weighing your candy, the cashier throws in an extra handful of candy. Read a book on crushing price objections, and the author throws in a bonus section on three additional and relevant topics.

Protecting your profitability is a blend of offensive and defensive strategies. Developing a discount discipline is part of it. This is your defensive strategy. Your strategy includes raising prices and getting the most from your bidding efforts. Part IV covers these three specific areas for protecting your profit.

By reading Part IV, taking notes, and studying the concepts, you will be able make better pricing decisions and protect your margins.

18

Developing a
Discount Discipline

In reading the lives of great men, I found that the first victory they
won was over themselves. Self-discipline with all of them came first.
—HARRY S TRUMAN

Discipline is bittersweet. We all know we need it, but we do not like the taste
of it. It comes partially from the fact that we often use it as a verb, which
frequently connotes punishment. As a noun, it sounds like a purposeful way
of doing things. In sales, the victory you win comes with and because of your
discipline—the noun, not the verb.

This chapter is about the type of discount discipline that helps you make
better seller decisions and to retain your profit from the sale. In this chapter,
you will learn

- eight realities of pricing;
- ten questions to ask yourself before discounting; and
- twenty-three discounting tips.

By studying these concepts and using them to make better pricing decisions,
you will become a successful guardian of your company's profit.

PRICING REALITIES

Making prudent pricing decisions is one of the toughest challenges facing sales and marketing professionals. Consider these eight realities:

1. Pricing drives profitability. According to McKinsey & Company, a 1 percent improvement in price yields about an 8 percent gain in operating profits. A 1 percent increase in selling price has three to four times the profit impact as the equivalent 1 percent increase in volume.

2. In the absence of all other indicators, price remains the number one indicator of quality. Buyers will see your price and make inferences about your quality. Higher priced goods invoke perceptions of higher quality. Lower priced goods evoke images of cheapness.

3. More than any sales and marketing campaign, your price tells the buyer how you feel about what you sell and what you believe it is worth. Price is how you communicate your belief about your value to the market. Thomas Paine's famous quote captures this point succinctly: "What we obtain too cheap, we esteem too lightly; it is dearness only that gives everything its value."

4. The discipline and courage you muster to engage price shoppers determine whether that relationship will be profitable for your company. Beyond the resolve to hold the line on your prices, this courage includes the discipline and willingness to know when to walk away.

5. Pricing is a strategic decision salespeople execute tactically. The correct price for your solution rests on the value it provides customers. A lack of discipline results in an arbitrary repositioning of the product or service by price-shopping buyers or by price-selling salespeople who lack the will or skill to stand by their value. Any movement of your price involves a repositioning of your brand.

6. One barrier to capturing full value from your proposition is a features-and-benefits mentality versus an outcome mentality. Features and benefits provide useful and necessary text for your product presentation. Outcome provides context for your value proposition. Your outcome is the result of your total customer experience.

7. Few companies have discount discipline or programmed pricing to secure the integrity of their margins. One study found that managers only spend about 10 percent of their time on pricing decisions. They spend more time studying costs than selling price. Does your company have a method for determining the discount you will give? What is your vetting process?

8. Some naive salespeople erroneously believe a discount is a one-shot deal while the buyer revels in how easy it was to get her price. Maybe it is the optimistic nature of salespeople to believe that they will not go through this again. Reality paints a different picture.

The discount vetting process in this chapter will give you the knowledge and skills that you need to strengthen your resolve and provide you with the information to make disciplined pricing decisions. Price authority without guidelines and accountability is foolish.

QUESTIONS TO ASK ABOUT DISCOUNTING

It may seem odd to include a section on discounting in a book that focuses on crushing price objections. The reality is, you will discount at some point. This section is damage control. Strategy is a coordinated and cohesive approach to challenges. To illustrate the importance of thinking strategically about pricing, see if you can answer these questions:

- What does your company want to do with its pricing program?
- What image does your company want to create in the market with its pricing program?
- What is your cost of goods?
- What is your cost of capital?

Why should you be able to make a decision that affects the profitability of your company if you cannot answer these questions or be held accountable for the profit impact of your decisions? When faced with a discount request, begin by asking yourself ten important questions so that your response, discounting or not, is strategic and not accidental.

Question #1: What Is Driving This Request?

Why is the buyer asking for a discount? This is information that you obtain from clarifying an objection. Is this request driven by internal forces like cost containment or external forces like market conditions? Is there a way other than discounting to meet the buyer's objective?

Question #2: Can This Be Sold More Profitably Somewhere Else?

If so, why sell it at a discounted price? Why sell discounted products to a price shopper and give away your profit when other buyers are willing to pay your price? The simple rules of supply and demand dictate that scarcity increases the perceived value of goods.

Question #3: How Much Pressure Is the Buyer Feeling?

In Chapter 2, you learned about buyer pressure points. Understanding his pressure points is part of shifting the buyer's focus off price and onto other relevant issues. If he needs to move on something in a hurry, price is less of an issue. If the buyer had a bad experience with your competition in the past, price should be less of an issue for you. As the buyer feels increasing pressure to buy your product, price becomes less important.

Question #4: Are We on an Irreversible, Precedent-Setting Course?

If you discount this time, will you do it every time this buyer orders in the future? Your discounted price becomes the new reference price for this buyer. Now that she knows you can and will discount, she may continue to ask for more concessions in the future. She may wield this precedent as part of her argument: "You worked with us in the past. What's changed?"

Question #5: Does This Action Start a Bigger Price War?

Will your competitors respond in kind to your discounting? Discounting in a mature market is different than discounting in a growth market. Buying a piece of business means your competitor will either match your price or undercut your price in another account to maintain their volume, and so the downward spiral begins. This does not justify discounting in a growth market; it explains that in a mature market, competitors have a stronger need to retaliate because of the shrinking market share potential.

Question #6: Will Our Trust Bond Be Broken?

Once you discount, it is a tacit admission that you have been charging too much all along. True or not, that is how the buyer interprets the move. You must be concerned about the trust bond you have established with this customer. Trust is the currency of good relationships. You do not want to squander it with a confusing pricing policy. This will arouse the buyer's suspicions in the future, too.

Question #7: Does Discounting Fit Our Overall Strategic Plan?

If so, it may be a good decision. If not, why would you want to do it? The key word in this question is *strategic*. Strategic means it is part of a larger and coordinated go-to-market plan. That is different from random acts of discounting. An example of strategic discounting is targeting a segment that carries a lower cost to serve. Because of a lower cost structure, your company may be price competitive in this narrow slice of the market. Another example may include lowering your price to secure volume for idled capacity. This may allow your company to spread costs over a broader expense base, protecting your profitability.

Question #8: Will We Resent the Business After We Get It?

There are countless stories of salespeople who took a piece of business and resented it afterward because they gave more than they got. If it is not equitable, it is not good business. Buyers who squeeze you on the front end for a better deal, demand more service than you anticipate, and pay late will destroy your bottom line. High-aggravation, low-margin, slow-paying buyers represent a segment of the market you want your competition to serve. Then you can take Napoleon's advice: "Never interrupt an enemy when he is making a mistake."

Question #9: Can We Afford to Invest Valuable Resources in a Price-Sensitive Account?

Unless your company has unlimited resources—and most companies do not—you must be selective in how you allocate your resources. Do you want to allocate precious resources to a price-sensitive buyer? Could you leverage these resources more profitably in another account? What happens if you commit your time and other resources to price-oriented buyers and it weakens your ability to serve more profitable customers or limits you from pursuing better opportunities? Discounting may end up being a bigger enemy than your competition.

Question #10: What Scares the Buyer More than Paying Too Much for Something?

In every sale, something concerns the buyer more than paying a higher price than he anticipated. That fear overshadows price. Understanding fear will help you negotiate better deals for your company. Fear, in this case, is an ally. In the chapter on proactive probing, there are a group of questions to help you spotlight fear and achieve a preemptive selling advantage.

DISCOUNTING TIPS

Discounting is a reality for most businesses. Making it more strategic than random and having a set of guidelines minimize the impact of lowering your price. The following list of suggestions will help you develop a discount discipline and protect your margins.

1. **To get serious about discounting, imagine it is your money that you are giving away.** Buyers are more protective of their own funds than they are of their companies' money. The converse of that is true also. Salespeople are less protective of their companies' money than their own money. Ask yourself, "What is the personal impact of this discount?"

2. **Do not use rounded discounts like 5, 10, 15, or 20 percent.** Use fractional discounts that have several digits to the right of the decimal point. For example, 4.76924 percent is better for you than 5 percent because you are retaining more profit and because all those digits to the right of the decimal tell the buyer this is as far as you can go.

3. **Avoid the question, "What is it going to take to make this deal happen?"** This is one of those questions that conjures negative images of slick salespeople. There are better ways to ask this question. For example, "What do

you recommend to move this forward?" or "What is our next step from here?" Leave the door open to discussions of matters other than discounting price.

4. When discounting individual items, scrutinize the cumulative profitability of the order. The synergy of product mix may yield greater profit than the sum of its individual items. Additionally, study the cash efficiency of the business. Will this order generate quicker cash flow and efficient inventory reduction?

5. Evaluate whether discounting changes your relationship with the customer. Will this discount contribute to a transaction-based relationship dominated by price discussions? A relationship-based sale is more focused on how you continue to bring value over the long term. Do you want to turn a good relationship into a transaction-based relationship?

6. It makes sense to do business with a price shopper only when there is a strategic advantage to that relationship. For example, price-sensitive buyers are useful when you have inventory to purge or discontinued items to unload. Price shoppers make sense when launching a value-stripped product at a lower price point. In this case, you have changed your value proposition. You have created something specifically for the price shopper.

7. Be careful when you attempt to buy a piece of business with penetration pricing. The market learns quickly about lower prices and adapts to them. Once you establish a reference price for the market and it stabilizes at that level, you must turn your focus inward to make additional profit from operational efficiency. This means profit comes from cutting something. You cannot cut your way to prosperity. You must grow your way to prosperity.

8. Discounting makes sense if it allows you to leverage your resources. As stated in Question #7 earlier in the chapter, idle capacity used to produce a flanking brand for a price-sensitive segment may be a prudent use of resources. Discounting a branded product to pursue that segment is a bad idea. You do not want to confuse the market with mixed value messages. For branded products, you do not want to turn a Rolex into a Timex.

9. Explore closing tools other than price that are available to you. Can you offer delivery as an option? What about extended warranty? Do you have flexibility with terms? Can you bundle training and onsite consultation into the package? In Chapter 16 on negotiating, I call the concessions that offer higher perceived value than your actual cost "funny money."

10. Remember the power of *free*. Buyers love this word. Marketers recognize its seductive powers in advertising. *Free* is better than a discount because it is a one-time deal. *Free* is an easier argument to make than discounting because it is part of your marketing strategy. *Free* never changes the reference price of goods. *Free* allows you to introduce a new product to buyers on a trial basis. *Free* gives you the opportunity to compete in a price-sensitive situation without changing your price.

For example, there is a candle store in a mall where we shop. I went in there to buy several scented candles. I asked the clerk if they ever went on sale, and she said, "No, but we do offer a seasonal promotion of four candles for the price of three. It is like getting one free!" They effectively gave me a 33 percent discount because I got one-third more product free, and the reference price never changed. Because I have more product to use, I am less likely to go to the competition for more candles, so it keeps me out of the competitor's store. How can the power of *free* work for your business?

11. Programmed pricing can add value to your discounting discipline. This means buyers must meet certain criteria clearly spelled out in your policies. This enables you to add the strength of systems to your price negotiation. It is a strong argument to fend off a price objection when the buyer knows you have this disciplined program in place and the only way to change the price is to meet the program criteria. One young salesman told me that it was a relief not to be able to negotiate price and use his company's programmed pricing as a way to deflect price objections. He said that it liberates him to spend most of the time selling his company's value versus seeking ways to shave a penny or two off the price.

12. Never discount your differentiator. When you cut price on a differentiator, it signals you do not fully believe in its value. The differentiator justifies your price. Why give away your competitive advantage in a price negotiation? If you offer a service plan as part of your bundle of value and the buyer asks you to throw it in at no charge, you effectively devalue your service plan. Why would the buyer want it if you attach no value to the differentiator?

13. If you must discount, cut something from your package to justify the price reduction. Otherwise, you are saying to the customer, "We were overcharging you all along." Remove the word *cut* from your vocabulary. Use *change* instead. For example, "Mr. Prospect, the only way for us to really change our price is if we change our package in some fashion." You are demonstrating that you are not cutting the price. You are changing the price because you are changing something about the package. This maintains your credibility.

You can get creative with this strategy by letting the buyer choose his price by changing the package: "We can let you choose your discount if you tell us what is not important to you and let us remove it from our package." This only works if your company is set up to sell cafeteria-style. Having buyers make trade-offs to change your price reinforces the value in your package. If you are not willing to stand up for your price, you settle for what the buyer wants to pay. You resent the deal, and the buyer is left wondering if he got the best price. He will test it again on the next order. Discounting never stops until you say no.

14. Ask the buyer for a longer commitment period as long as it is not a net price. If it is a percentage discount off a published price and you can live with that percentage over a period of time, ask the buyer for a three-year commitment versus a one-year commitment. This helps you avoid going through this negotiation again. Price shoppers make transactional, short-term decisions. Buyers wanting to partner will commit to long-term relationships. Their willingness to agree to this is a measure of their commitment to the relationship.

15. Ask for more business, especially in areas where you know you have high-margin products. A broader mix of products helps compensate for the loss on lower-margin items. When studying items for discounting, consider inventory turns. Some inventory turns quickly with lower carrying costs. Some inventory turns more slowly and suffers higher carrying costs. Consider dead inventory as part of your negotiated discount. The bigger discount applies only to the dead inventory and ceases when the inventory is depleted.

16. Be selective and limit the discount. Buyers cherry-pick. This means they select items from vendors that offer them the lowest price. Sellers can do this as well. Be selective. Limit the discount to specific areas where you can absorb the hit and recoup profit in other areas.

17. Use time to your advantage. Have a kill date for special net pricing so the buyer does not think this is open-ended. This creates a positive sense of urgency and finality to the discount. Also, it protects you from cost increases beyond the kill date.

18. Can you offer a lump-sum discount versus a line-item discount?
Assume you have six line items on an invoice. If you show a lump-sum discount on the bottom of the invoice for all six items versus a line-item discount, you have done two things. First, it has greater visual impact to see a bigger number at the bottom of the invoice. Second, it protects the reference price of the individual line items on top of the invoice. The message is straightforward: the buyer gets this discount only if he purchases this mix and quantity.

19. Offer a skewed discount. This means the more a customer buys, the higher the discount. It stairsteps the discount. Instead of a fixed discount regardless of volume, a skewed discount increases as the customer buys more volume. This protects you against the buyer who promises to buy more but falls short of ordering all that he has promised.

For a serious buyer, an accelerated discount delivers exactly what he wants. For example, if a buyer commits to purchasing $100,000 worth of material, offer a higher discount when he reaches the $80,000 level. This progressively higher discount protects your margins.

20. Offer year-end rebates versus discounts. When you rebate, offer credits toward future purchases, not cash. Giving away credit toward future goods is a better deal for your company because your cost of goods is lower than your cost of money. Because the customer must buy more to use the rebate, it guarantees future business. For loyal, repeat customers, this is a win-win option.

21. Change price only after you have a firm commitment from the buyer. Otherwise, the buyer will use your discounted price to drive down the competitor's price. Do not give the buyer negotiating leverage to use with your competition. Say to the buyer, "Ms. Buyer, I will pursue this with my management to see if there is anything we can do, but the first question they will ask is, 'Is the buyer serious? Do we have a firm commitment on their part to move forward if we find common ground?' Will you commit to that?"

If the buyer refuses, you know she was shopping price, not negotiating in good faith. If the buyer is serious, a firm commitment is no problem. Ask for the commitment, and if she fails to commit, you have lost nothing because you never had the business.

22. Dig for the discount it will take to get the order. Ask the buyer these two questions. The wording on these questions is critical.

- ▪ **Question #1: "What do you have in mind?"** Do not say, "Tell me what you *need*." Instead, you may ask the following: "Tell me what you want." "Tell me what you have in mind." "Tell me your *target* price." These sound flexible from the buyer's perspective, and *need* sounds absolute, a must-have.
- ▪ **Question #2: "Do you care how I get you there?"** This is the key question. When the buyer says no, it opens the door for alternate ways you can help her achieve her target price. Implicit in this question is that you will change your package to meet what she is willing to pay.

23. Use a special pricing action. A special pricing action sounds better than a discount or cutting your price. Watch your wording. When you discuss changing price or adjusting price, you are warning that you may change or adjust the package to justify changing the price. This is similar to Tip #13. A special pricing action indicates a one-time deal. It is a transaction-specific discount designed to address a special situation. It describes a one-time buying opportunity.

CHAPTER SUMMARY

It is vital to develop a discount discipline, a strategic rather than random approach to pricing. Random acts of discounting are like death by a thousand knife cuts. Put discipline in your pricing strategy; be tightfisted and selective with discounts; and be a guardian of your margins and protector of your profitability. You learned eight realities about discounting, ten important questions to ask before discounting, and twenty-three tips for more effective discounting. By developing this discount discipline, asking yourself the right questions before changing your price, and planning your strategy, you can protect the lifeblood of your organization—profit.

19

Raising Prices

Fortune befriends the bold.

—JOHN DRYDEN, ENGLISH POET AND PLAYWRIGHT

Few things frighten salespeople more than raising prices. This may be one of the most important things you do this year but the thing you fear most. A greater fear than raising prices when needed should be not raising them when needed. What could be more compelling than realizing you are delaying capturing the value your company needs to operate competitively and serve customers well?

This chapter is about doing what you know you must do: raising prices. You can raise prices and extract more value from the market, and the following information presented in this chapter will help you:

- Five attitudes that will help you decide what you must do
- Why, when, and how to raise prices
- Fifteen ways to present price increases to customers

By studying these concepts and using them to understand the importance and appropriateness of raising prices, you will be able to design a strategy and present this successfully to customers.

THE POWER OF FEAR

Fear is a red-hot emotion and an incredibly powerful motivating and demotivating force. We are hardwired to detect danger, and when we do, the fear center in the brain activates, and we engage in predictably irrational fight-or-flight behavior. Fear is such a dominant emotion that it overpowers most other emotions. People will forego gain to avoid fear. This is why individuals and organizations delay raising prices for as long as they can. Consider this:

- You have held prices firm.
- You are being squeezed to hold your costs down though they are rising.
- You have done everything possible internally to operate more efficiently.
- The competition is aggressively pursuing your market share.
- Customers are demanding more for less.
- The pressure on your bottom line is relentless.

What should you do?

Not raising prices foretells costing yourself out of business, and raising prices threatens market share. Is there any doubt why two-thirds of small businesses failed to raise prices during the most recent period of economic prosperity? They feared a loss of market share more than loss of profit. Something is incredibly wrong with that picture.

How many customers do you serve who value your goods and services by a factor greater than what they now currently pay? If you are locked into a volume mindset, you fear losing share more than profit. Most companies fear elasticity in their pricing, in particular, demand dropping as prices increase. This is a direct outcome of market-share mania—the obsession with share over profit. Profit is the metric you take to the bank, not share. The relationship is more complex than this, but I am trying to make a point. If you fear losing business more than losing profit, you will fail to raise prices as needed.

You cannot absorb higher costs forever. Sooner or later, you must pass these along to the market. Those who absorb too much of the increase will absorb themselves into weakness: fewer resources to invest, less flexibility in strategy, and less return to investors. Failing to pass along increases while absorbing them yourself is effectively discounting your goods to the market. Compound this with customers who demand greater value for a lower price, and how many ways can you discount and remain in business?

In the previous chapter, the focus was on how to develop a discount discipline and retain profit. This defensive strategy sought to prevent further erosion by making better seller decisions when the buyer asks for a lower price. The focus of this chapter is to protect your profit by adjusting prices. This offensive strategy of adjusting prices is part of a broader effort on your part to retain profitability and remain viable in your market. That broader effort has been the theme throughout this book. Adjusting your prices to reflect volatile market conditions is part of this.

HEALTHY ATTITUDES ABOUT PRICE INCREASES

Since fear is a powerful motivator, you can balance its effects with a healthy set of attitudes. People move in the direction of their thoughts, and they become what they think about. The following attitudes create fertile soil for your efforts to sustain and grow profitability.

Attitude #1: We Are a For-Profit Organization

Unless your company is truly a nonprofit organization, you must earn a profit every year. That money is reinvested in your organization to improve your competitive position by increasing value to the customer and to provide a stable environment for employees. Your compensation and future depends on your company's profitability. Being compensated equitably is an organizational and individual issue.

Attitude #2: We Deserve to Be Compensated for Our Value-Added Services

If you provide a value-added solution that has a positive impact on your customer, you deserve to be compensated for it. That is the definition of equity. Price is what they pay; value is what they receive. Delivering value means your solution exceeds the price they pay. It is a fair exchange for the customer. Anything short of capturing return value is not equitable.

Your sense of fairness and desire for equity should overshadow your fear of losing the business. If fear dominates your thinking, you will act to avoid versus acting to acquire or gain. Acting to avoid puts you in a defensive mode. It is difficult to gain traction if you are acting defensively. You are playing not to lose.

Attitude #3: Profit Is an Important Part of Future Growth and Stability

Your company cannot grow without a strong bottom line. Your company cannot offer customers stability in the future without a stable bottom line. Customers who want a long-term relationship with a supplier realize the supplier's financial welfare is a building block for the future. Buyers who look only at the transaction could not care less if your future is questionable; they only care about now. Is that the foundation upon which to build your business?

Attitude #4: Customers Want to Deal with Organizations That Are Prepared for the Future

What good is it for a customer to buy from a supplier with no promise of future stability? What good is a product warranty with no assurance the supplier will be there to support it? Customers want to partner with stable organizations. They want to sleep at night knowing the supplier will be there when they need them. Customers need partners who continue to innovate and reinvest in their businesses. Who wants to place his future in the hands of a seller who will not safeguard his own interests? If a seller will not look out for himself, why would he look out for the customer?

Attitude #5: We Are Managing Value

Are you raising prices or managing value? Managing value ensures you create win-win outcomes. You and the customer must gain from this relationship. Managing pricing is managing value, which maintains profitability. The key to price optimization is charging for the value you deliver. This fair exchange is fundamental to companies operating profitably. It is the foundation of equity in your relationships.

COMPANIES RAISE PRICES FOR A NUMBER OF REASONS

Understanding why companies raise prices will help you with your decisions and strategy. Asking *why* instead of *how* is a better way to begin to design a strategy.

  1. **Companies raise prices to capture lost ground or catch up.** Maybe it has been too long since the company raised prices and it has absorbed as much increase as it can. It is time to get well.

2. Companies raise prices to stop the bleeding. If raw material prices go up, companies raise prices to adjust to the market. Your customers do this also. You cannot absorb material costs indefinitely. This makes your increase a pricing adjustment.

3. Companies raise prices because the timing is right. There may never be a better time to raise prices. The economy may be strong enough that most customers will not respond negatively to a price increase. Some of them may be passing increases along to their customers.

4. Companies raise prices because it creates a natural selection process for certain customers. Raising prices enables companies to target certain customers, thinning the ranks. This is especially effective with profit piranhas—customers that chew away at your profitability. Unprofitable, price-shopping customers will set their sights on your competition. Raising prices will expedite the exodus from your company.

WHEN TO RAISE PRICES

After deciding why to raise prices, it's important to ask when.

▪ **Use bandwagon increases.** Raise prices when everybody else does. It provides cover and diversion. You see this in the stock market when entire segments of an industry announce bad news together. These executives take cover in everyone else's bad news.

▪ **When customers do well.** Customers experiencing rapid growth are less price sensitive because they are more focused on their top line sales. The opposite happens when their top line retreats; they turn their attention to the bottom line, and you experience more price resistance.

▪ **With positive news.** When there is an increase in the consumer price index or any other meaningful reference standard that provides financial justification, it provides an opportunity for you to frame the increase within the context of a positive economic backdrop. When the economy is steaming forward, what better time to raise prices? Most suppliers and customers will follow this same course.

▪ **When demand changes.** Increase prices when demand increases. As demand increases, supply becomes scarcer, and Economics 101 teaches you to never underprice scarce resources. Greater demand than supply means you protect your prices and profit. The opposite applies, too. Lower demand than supply challenges your prices and profitability.

■ **With no push-back.** If you are not getting a lot of price resistance from customers, you may not be charging enough. One telltale sign is that you are outgrowing the competition and doing nothing special to get the business. If your closing ratio takes off and you are not selling any differently, buyers see the value in your proposition and want to take advantage of it. Test the market with a price increase and see what happens.

■ **As costs increase.** Companies raise prices as costs increase. This is especially true in volatile, commodity, raw-materials industries. Customers may not like it, but they understand. You have done everything on your end to become operationally efficient and may be stronger for these efforts. Now, it is time for customers to share in the inevitable increases that accompany volatile markets.

■ **With package designs.** Change price when you repackage or bundle your products differently. As you add value to your package, your prices must reflect this or buyers take the enhancements for granted. Product enhancements—the new and improved version—allow companies to raise prices. Accompanying these changes in packages must be a change in the buyer's perception of your value. Change the package and change the perceived value. Then, you can adjust the price.

■ **For target growth.** As your customer base expands and you want to limit that customer base or restrict sales to certain segments, you can raise prices to select those customers who will be most profitable. This is selective growth. Some will stay; some will leave.

■ **As competition dwindles.** Raise prices as you experience declining competition. This happens in markets that have gone through maturity. As suppliers abandon the market, the remaining suppliers are able to raise their prices to reflect a smaller supply side. You may discover targeted opportunities if niche players fade, and you can pick up market share in these segments.

■ **On schedule.** Raise prices at the beginning of a time period. It could be an industry paradigm that January 1 brings new prices. Your industry may adjust prices quarterly. Some may adjust monthly, weekly, or daily. If you are tied to the commodities markets, your prices change constantly.

HOW TO ADJUST PRICES

Once you have asked and answered why and when to raise prices, you must address how to raise prices. To respond to this question, you must target customers and products.

Question #1: Will We Raise Prices for Everyone?

Are you going to raise prices across the board, in other words, across all customer segments, or target specific segments of the market for price increases? Are some segments willing and able to absorb the increases because their market conditions are different and they can extract more value from your package? Never assume because some segments are struggling that all segments are struggling.

Revisiting your value proposition is a part of adjusting prices. Your value proposition affects you and the customer. Are there unprofitable customers for whom you could reduce the number of services you offer them to lower your costs? These customers are profit piranhas. Can you lower your costs to serve profit piranhas and improve your overall profit before raising your prices?

Adjusting prices for customers could be as simple as enforcing payment terms. Some customers take advantage of your payment terms without honoring them. Unless you are in the banking business, there is no reason for you to carry their debt. Close the door on this practice, and your bottom line will improve.

Question #2: Will We Raise Prices for All of Our Products or Cherry-Pick Certain Ones?

Is this pricing adjustment necessary because of across-the-board increases or targeted increases? Your analysis may uncover that across-the-board increases are unnecessary at this point. When across-the-board cuts are necessary, some customers may interpret your move as an attempt to gain ground on your margins.

Question #3: If We Raise Prices in Some Areas Because of Cost Increases, Are There Areas Where We Will Lower Prices Because of Cost Decreases?

This is a natural follow-up to the second question. Mitigating price increases in certain areas with decreases in others presents a compelling argument, as customers witness an even-handed approach. Consider the impact of your approaching the customer with an increase-decrease announcement.

Question #4: Do We Need to Raise the Price on Ancillaries?

Ancillaries include all the things that surround your sales and operations: freight, packaging, delivery, installation, and training. When increasing prices, you should focus on your core business. Charging freight is a legitimate cost of doing business and not a profit center unless you are in that industry. When buyers become aware that you are raising associated costs like freight as a way to extract more value from them, they get irritated, and rightly so. There are some pass-through expenses that should go directly to customers without adding to them.

Handling and packaging expenses for standard orders raise the ire of buyers. How can you sell without handling and packaging? That should be built into your base cost. Peeling off this cost may satisfy the auditors, but it irritates the customers.

Some companies surreptitiously raise prices by increasing minimum orders, begin charging for delivery, and charge more for special packaging. These stealth increases may not draw the overwhelming attention that across-the-board increases draw, and you can present a compelling argument for this action.

Question #5: Can We Use Cafeteria-Style Pricing?

Some companies raise prices cafeteria-style. They charge for value-added services and let customers choose the ones they want.

Some companies launch an upscale version of a product and increase the price of the upscale product. Other companies raise prices by changing the packaging. Instead of packaging twenty-four items in a case, they now package it twenty per case but leave the price alone. The price did not change, but the package changed.

How to raise prices targets customers and products. There is no one answer to this question that fits all circumstances. Studying your needs within the context of customer needs will provide some answers for you. This approach seems customer friendly, and it is. The problem is that your cost structure may be spread across all orders and services. Before opting for cafeteria-style pricing, sales and operations must talk about the overall impact of this approach.

HOW TO PRESENT YOUR PRICE INCREASE

You have decided that it is time to adjust prices, planned how to do it, and identified which customers will be affected. Your next question is, "How do I present this information to customers?"

Tip #1: Words Matter

When you present the price increase, present it as an *adjustment* or *change* based on market conditions. Make it clear you are not raising prices to raise margins. You are raising prices to remain profitable. Customers are resistant to suppliers who are simply trying to make more money when they raise prices.

Reference the consumer price index or another accepted standard increase since your original contract with the customer. Show that you are keeping up with inflation, not gaining ground on margins. This reference standard deflects the buyer's frustration to industry forces and legitimizes your response.

The words you choose can make a big difference. Referring to commodity prices and raw materials shifts the focus from your profit to market variables. When you lump together several of these costs, use a metric that makes sense to customers. For example, a printer must consider the cost of paper, ink, the energy to run the presses, rent, and labor expense. The figure that he uses to quantify this might be "cost per sheet of printing." This number may reflect a combination of fixed and variable expenses, exhibiting the increase across several variables.

When costs increase, adjusting prices is a sound business decision. Buyers may not like it, but they respect your thought process and business model. Choose words carefully and build your case methodically. A cohesive response to changing market challenges tells buyers your company has a viable go-to-market strategy and a pricing model based on integrity.

Tip #2: Be Clear on and Communicate Your Motivation

Tell the customer that you have delayed long enough. You are not overcharging now; you have been undercharging until now. This leaves room for you to demonstrate how much of the cost your company has already absorbed before passing it along. You are sharing the rest of the increase with the customer. You have done everything you can do on your end to absorb the increase through greater efficiencies. You are passing through a cost over which you have no control—the cost of raw materials. You have been able to hold the increase to a minimum. For you to continue to hold the prices at the current level is bad business. Customers understand this.

The buyer's perception of fairness has much to do with your motivation to raise prices. Gaining ground with an increase is a recipe for conflict when the customer gets wind of it. Fairness is subjective. When you add to the buyer's suspicion with fuzzy wording, no increase or adjustment will seem fair. Remind customers you value their business and understand firsthand the pain they are experiencing. It opens the door for your adjustment discussions.

Tip #3: Provide Context

Document how your costs for materials, labor, or energy have increased. These are signpost items that buyers use to judge inflation. The cost of food and gasoline are relevant analogies. Even if these do not have a direct bearing on the products you sell, it provides context to explain your adjustment. Include in writing a few of these increases to demonstrate the larger picture. The objective is to add context to the broader discussion of rising costs, not to obscure increases in your price.

Ironically, when customers complain that their costs have increased in other areas, they are providing you with the ideal context to discuss your adjustments. When the buyer tells you he needs a 5 percent decrease, you can argue persuasively you are struggling with how to keep the increase to 5 percent. This is a strong argument for you to make, but it legitimizes your increase.

Tip #4: Cost Decrease

Demonstrate how a price increase results in a cost decrease for the customer because of your solution's impact on his business. This presumes your downline value supports this. Encouraging the buyer to take a long-term view opens the door for your lower-cost argument. This becomes a good-news, bad-news conversation. Be prepared to roll out your chronology of value demonstrating the economic impact on the buyer's costs.

Tip #5: Present the Adjustment in Person

When raising prices for key customers, a face-to-face conversation is better than an impersonal letter. Go to your better customers first for their reaction. You cannot gauge their reaction on the phone or by written notice. You must be accessible and visible during this period to reassure buyers, listen to them, and answer their questions. With new customers, present your increase matter-of-factly, as standard operating procedure.

Tip #6: Present the Whole Thing

Present the price adjustment against a backdrop of value. This strategy involves a value-reminding campaign. Summarize all of the value that you have brought to the customer and its impact on their company. Then, give the buyer a preview of all you will do for them going forward. This reiterates your commitment to serve the buyer.

Tip #7: The Best Defense Is a Good Offense

Launch a defensive selling campaign prior to your price increases. At ninety days before an increase, initiate a campaign to review the impact your solution has had on the customer's business. This is similar to Tip #6, except the reminding begins in advance of the increase.

I met a salesman who recorded his buyer's positive comments about his company for two years prior to an increase and used these written comments as the first page of a price-increase notice. He told me that the buyer said he remembered everything the salesperson recorded, and the price increase went through smoothly.

Tip #8: Give Some Breathing Room

Offer key customers a grandfather clause that extends their adjustment period. This adjustment period allows them to prepare their market for the increases. Offer this in lieu of discounting the increase. Anytime you discount the increase, you lose ground. For example, assume your price increase is 6 percent, but with key customers you limit it to 4 percent. You have discounted the increase by a third. You will need to make up that concession with your next increase. Discounting an increase is no different from discounting your current price. The only difference is that you are giving away profit you have not captured yet. The next increase will need to be higher to capture the profit you gave away during the previous increase. How long can this go on?

Tip #9: Sell the Increase Internally

Managers, this tip is especially for you. Before you can pass on this increase to the customers, you must sell your salespeople on the importance of this increase. If they do not believe in the increase, they will not convince the customer it is necessary. The ways you sell the increase externally are the same ideas you will use to sell this adjustment to your staff. Enlist their support through understanding, and they will become credible champions of the adjustment.

Tip #10: Do Not Apologize for the Increase

When you apologize, it demonstrates a lack of conviction on your part. The buyer perceives this as a sign that he may be able to discourage you by holding fast to his position that he will not accept the increase. You can express regret for having to take this action and acknowledge the buyer's frustration, but do not apologize for making a sound business decision. Why should you apologize for your company earning a profit?

If you refer back to Chapter 9 on how to present your prices, the same principles apply to presenting an increase. You want to project confidence and conviction. The buyer must perceive that he or she is dealing with a business-person who understands the economics of running a business. This knowledge, coupled with an understanding of your customer's cost structure, can help you present a compelling argument for the price adjustment.

Tip #11: Sell Financially

Use financial selling tips to minimize the increase. If it is a 5 percent increase, what does that mean in real dollars? Can you minimize the impact by breaking down this price difference into a small and meaningful unit? Five percent may sound higher than six cents per unit or four cents per hour. Spotlight the increases only, not the total cost. If it is a 5 percent increase, break down the actual difference between the old and new price into the smallest yet most meaningful unit, and if it compares favorably with other materials the buyer is purchasing, draw an analogy to those items. Your increase may seem small by comparison.

Tip #12: Float a Trial Balloon

Some companies float a trial balloon to test their increases. This negotiating technique tests buyer sensitivity and resistance before the actual adjustment. It is spreading a rumor that this may happen and checking the reaction of the market. Another advantage of the trial balloon is that it softens the buyer's mind for when the increase actually happens. Additionally, if the real increase is smaller than the buyer heard through the grapevine, he may feel relieved. I am not suggesting you intentionally mislead buyers with a higher trial balloon. If you study their reaction and respond appropriately, the increase may be smaller or higher.

Tip #13: Everyone Pays the Piper

Buyers perceive increases to be fair if everyone must abide by the new prices. Favoritism fuels discontent. When you can honestly say everyone will absorb this increase, it strengthens your case and increases the probability the increase will stick. No one has an advantage over another, which is especially important with smaller companies because they believe larger companies have an advantage in this area. Tell them it is a level playing field and you are protecting everyone equally. Some customers who resent the idea that they do not receive special consideration will respect the fact that no one else does either. That builds trust.

Tip #14: Use Your Champions

Enlist the aid of champions to grease the skids for the price adjustment. You may find the greatest support comes from the people who use your product. They understand its value and want to protect your position with their financial buyer or purchasing representative. As they create pull to get you into the account, they can reinforce your value to keep you in the account. If the only people you call on are in purchasing, their perspectives are mostly logistics. Others involved in the decision may appreciate the efficiency, competitive advantage, or quality your product represents. For them, the price increase may seem small and necessary to sustain your value. Their input can balance the logistics buyer's concern over price.

Tip #15: Anticipate Push-Back

Expect buffeting. Some buyers comply with little fuss. Some will gripe and go along, and others will explode and threaten your business with them. Buyers who know more about your products and the benefits are less price sensitive. Informed buyers understand. Be prepared for resistance but do not create it. Preparation for resistance lowers your risk of caving in.

CHAPTER SUMMARY

Salespeople can mitigate the fear they have about price increases through better planning and more effective execution. Companies raise prices for a number of reasons—to recover lost profit, pass along materials increases, or selectively screen customers. In this chapter, you learned five important attitudes about price increases, the upside and downside of raising prices, how and when to do it, and fifteen tips to present this increase to customers. Price increases need not be the anxiety-filled experience most salespeople anticipate. Planning and preparation help. Understand why your increases are necessary and work on how you will present this information to customers. You can retain your profitable relationships with customers as costs increase.

20

Competitive Bidding

Competition is the keen cutting edge of business, always shaving
away at costs.

—HENRY FORD

The most benign interpretation of competitive bids is that buyers want to
ensure they receive the most and the best for the least. This appeals to the
buyer in all of us and annoys the seller in most of us. Buyers request bids, hoping the threat of competition will cause sellers to shave away as much margin
as possible. It reminds me of a director of purchasing who once said to a group
of salespeople: "My job is to chisel you out of as much margin as I can. Your
job is to not let me do my job." Simple and straightforward advice. Competitive
bidding makes your job tougher but not impossible.

This chapter is about operating profitably in a bid environment. You can
retain profitability if you have a strategy for competitive bidding. This strategy
will involve many of the concepts presented in this chapter:

- Your rights as a salesperson
- Developing a bidding strategy for bid preparation, bid submission, and
  afterward
- Deciding if you want to participate in online bids and auctions

By studying competitive bidding, you will be able to maximize your results if
you decide to include this as part of your go-to-market strategy.

SALESPERSON'S BILL OF RIGHTS

It has been my experience that most salespeople are intimidated by the buyer when quoting something. Part of the reason is that you do not fully understand your rights in that situation. This is your "bill of rights" as a salesperson:

Right #1: You Have the Right to All Information and Decision-Maker Input That Is Vital to Your Bid

Before the quote, you are entitled to talk with all relevant parties (decision makers) who will be involved in the selection process. Otherwise, your bid is a shot in the dark. If you were a doctor, would you prescribe without seeing the patient? No. If the buyer denies you the opportunity, use that analogy to drive home your request to meet with everyone involved and affected by the bid, including end users of the product or service you are selling. Common sense is on your side. If the buyer is uncooperative before the sale, can you imagine how uncooperative he will be after the sale? No price is good enough! No delivery is soon enough! No service is good enough! If you lose business from an uncooperative buyer, console yourself with the question, do you really want this type of business?

One major advantage of engaging all influencers is that it gives you a complete picture of their needs. This helps shape your bid. Also, you have the opportunity to reinforce your uniqueness with influencers.

Right #2: You Have a Right to Know the Selection Criteria Used in the Final Decision

Would you gamble your money in a Las Vegas card game without knowing the rules? Of course not. In sales, when you do not know the rules before you quote, you are gambling with your time and margins. Find out in advance the relative importance of price, delivery, responsiveness, and technical support. Ask the buyer this question: "Once all bids are submitted, what is your decision process and how will you arrive at that decision?" You are entitled to know this.

Right #3: You Have a Right to Know with Whom You Are Competing

Explain to the buyer that you expect nothing more than the same courtesy she would expect from her customers. Explain that you are interested in maintaining your margins while offering a fair deal, and you need some competitive information to do that. Your justification is to help the buyer. This information will help you design your bid so the differences in value are more apparent to her, making her decision easier.

Right #4: You Have a Right to a Recap After the Contract Is Awarded

Explain to the buyer that one of your conditions is that you receive at least an oral summary of how you compared with other bidders. You may not get specific numbers, but you may get a range. Tell the buyer this feedback is part of your company's marketing strategy.

Gather as much information as possible during this recap: how the competition bid, what they bid, prices, options, or any difference in their strategy from previous bids. This systematic recap is then given to your marketing department as competitive intelligence. When the entire sales force systematically debriefs customers after the bid, your company can amass solid information about the market and changes in competitor's strategies.

If any of these personal rights seem extreme or aggressive to you, consider the alternative. You are called into a buyer's office because he wants you to quote a price on something. Since you have not called here much in the past, you are unsure of their needs. You ask permission to speak to some of the end users but are declined permission. The buyer tells you everything is handled through him. He gives you scanty information about their needs and cannot answer technical questions that give you a strategic advantage in bidding. When you ask what selection criteria he uses for buying decisions, he says, "The usual: price, quality, and delivery!" The buyer then informs you that there are two other vendors competing with you but fails to tell you who they are. In his words, "Our policy is not to tell you who you are competing with. Just give us your best price, and we will let you know if you win!" When you ask about the bid recap, the buyer says all you will know is who won and nothing more.

If the buyer treats you this way going into a quote, you know how he will treat you after you get the business. Are you sure you want to do business with him? Is the aggravation factor worth the profit? You have rights as a salesperson. When you do not respect yourself, buyers will not respect you. If you believe in your rights and assert them, buyers will respect you as a businessperson.

BIDDING STRATEGY

When you receive a request for quotation, you must have a strategy. Divide your strategy into three parts: before the quote, submitting the quote, and recapping your quote.

Before the Quote

The negotiated settlement is better for both parties because the in-depth discussions that accompany negotiations are missing in a bid situation. Ask the buyer this question: "What do you hope to achieve with a bid that you cannot get in working with us one-on-one?" We examined this strategy in the chapter on dealing with procedural-based money objections. If the buyer tells you she still must bid, be clear on her decision criteria.

Discover if the buyer plans to bid without suggesting she bid by asking these questions, "Tell me about your decision process" or "How will you make your decision?" Or "What factors will go into your buying decision?" If the buyer tells you she will put this business out for bid, try for the negotiated settlement. Ask this question, "What do you hope to accomplish with a bid that you cannot get working with us one on one?"

Determine the actual buying authority before you submit your quote. Find out who will have impact on the decision and visit with them before you bid. Understand their needs from the top floor to the shop floor. If board approval is part of the procedure, meet with individual board members. Develop some loyalties. Establish strong allies on the board who will champion your cause. This person(s) can be your sounding board for feedback.

Try to get the buyer to write the quote according to your specifications. This works well when your product has unique advantages over the competition. You can engineer this when you gain thorough account penetration with end users.

Gather relevant information. Standardize this information by developing a fact sheet containing the following information:

- Selection criteria for products and vendors.
- Timetable for decision making and delivery of the products and services.
- Information regarding your competition for this piece of business.
- Bidding history of this account. For example, who got this business in the past and at what level? Did the buyer order as much as he originally stated in the quote? How satisfied is the buyer with previous suppliers? How do terms affect the buying decision? Does the supplier's location make a difference to the buyer?

When designing your proposal, make it as unique as possible. Use quality binding. Begin with a summary of the buyer's needs. Include a cover sheet with a confidentiality clause to protect your work. This keeps honest people honest.

Expand the section of no-charge items; it creates a perception of higher value. Include guarantees and testimonials. Be sure to demonstrate how your product specifically addresses the buyer's needs. Put a time limit on the quote to avoid delays.

Submitting the Quote

▪ If possible, deliver the proposal in person so you can answer questions that surface.

▪ Begin by reviewing the buyer's needs, get agreement to those needs, and demonstrate how your solution satisfies those needs.

▪ Sell the buyer on the total, long-term value of your solution.

▪ Elaborate on the no-charge items and stress the guarantees you offer.

▪ Ask subtle questions to elicit immediate feedback on how your solution compares with the competition.

▪ Seek active buyer involvement throughout the presentation to draw out concerns or doubts.

▪ Explain how you arrived at your price.

▪ Ask for the order.

Recapping Your Quote

▪ Get feedback immediately following the bid award.

▪ Talk to as many people as possible. Sometimes an end user paints a much different picture than the buyer.

▪ Pinpoint the selection criteria used to make the decision.

▪ Discover who got the bid and at what price level.

▪ Ask the buyer, "What could we have done differently to earn your business?"

▪ Send a recap letter to the buyer thanking him for the opportunity to quote. Reaffirm your interest in his business, and inform him you will continue to call for future opportunities.

▪ Schedule follow-up calls to determine the buyer's satisfaction with the other supplier. Determine the competition's ability to meet the buyer's needs, both present and future.

Quoting does not need to be a painful or intimidating situation. Have a strategy for your proposals, and go the extra step to make your proposal or bid unique. If you do not get the business, maintain periodic contact, because you might identify other business at higher profitability than your original quote.

IF YOU LOSE THE BID

What happens if you lose the bid? Do you withdraw your bid? These options are open to you at this point:

- Use the safety-net strategy. Offer to hold your prices firm for thirty days, and tell the buyer you want to be his safety net during this transition period. Be clear the offer is good for only thirty days.
- You could offer to become an alternate source. You may raise your prices slightly to reflect the lower volume, but tell the buyer you would like to be his backup source if he wants you.
- Another option is to raise your prices fully and continue to call on the buyer and wait for the competition to fail.

One of the most creative strategies I have seen came from the owner of a small company. His buyer requested he bid on a service contract for one year. The competition's bid was full of loopholes, which enabled them to quote a lower bid price. The buyer gave my client the opportunity to meet the competitor's bid. My client decided not to play the game and responded by saying, "What I would really like to do is to help you fix this bid. If you accept this as is, you are going to find yourself in a situation in which you are not getting what you need. I would like to withdraw my bid completely from this job and become your consultant to help you fix this bid. I am not doing this to get the business. All I am asking is that when it comes time for the next contract, I want to negotiate with you one-on-one versus your bidding the next project."

The buyer agreed. They plugged the holes, and the competition had to redo some things. It saved the buyer headaches, and my client got the next piece of business without bidding.

ONLINE BIDS

Online bidding and reverse auctions represent a special challenge for salespeople. An online bid, sometimes referred to as a reverse auction, means that buyers will use the Internet to conduct a live auction. They begin with a target price, and bidders submit their prices below the target price. That's why it is a reverse auction. The price goes lower, not higher. Buyers use this method so that sellers can see what their competition is bidding. The theory is that it will drive prices lower, and it generally does. They can represent good business if this fits your overall strategy. When faced with this business decision, ask these five questions:

■ Do I want or really need this type of business, knowing it is strictly price-driven?
■ How much energy do I want to put into this low-margin business?
■ What is the impact of this low-margin business on my other customers and my ability to serve them?
■ Is my company set up to handle this type of business? Do we have an infrastructure in place that is built on operational efficiency that enables us to sell profitably to price shoppers?
■ Do we have inventory we want to dump, and is this a good place to do it?

Before you decide online bidding and reverse auctions are places you want to invest a lot of time, ask this fundamental question: "Is this good business for our company?"

CHAPTER SUMMARY

A common attitude about competitive bidding is that you cannot profit from it. You can if you are willing to put some energy into it. Understanding your rights and having a strategy that carries you from request to award helps protect your margins. There are instructive questions you can ask yourself before you bid online. Your challenge going forward is to prepare for bids. Talk to your marketing department, and create a bid fact sheet and recap sheet. As you and your peers compile this intelligence and share it internally, your company can develop a winning strategy.

21

Final Thoughts

I shall be telling this with a sigh
Somewhere ages and ages hence:
Two roads diverged in a wood, and I—
I took the one less traveled by,
And that has made all the difference.
—ROBERT FROST, FROM "THE ROAD NOT TAKEN"

This book has been about which road you will travel—the one to price reduction or the one to profit enhancement. I wrote this book to encourage and empower you to choose the road to profit retention and growth. Ultimately, this is your decision. Price objections do not necessarily signal the end of the road or even the end of the sale. Remember, the sale is never over until you or the customer quits the journey.

There are some recurring themes running throughout this book to reinforce basic selling principles:

- Price objections are a daily reality for salespeople. Despite your best efforts, you will encounter them.
- Your attitude about your prices affects your profitability.
- Crushing price objections is more than simply defending your prices; it is about protecting your margins and retaining your profit.

■ Equity is the foundation of good business relationships.

■ There is some business you want to walk away from and some you want to pursue. Your ability to discern the two will make all the difference in the world.

■ Value is more than a cheap price. It is an outcome for the buyer.

■ You may fight the battle in the buyer's mind, but the buyer is not your enemy. Your real opponent is the thought process that causes people to decide on price alone.

■ The critical success factor in holding the line on price is your preparation. As you never want to be outsold by the competition, you never want to be out-prepared by the customer for the price negotiation.

■ The two fundamental strategies that link all the strategies and tactics in this book are *stretching the buyer's time horizon* and *enlarging the conversation*.

■ You can achieve a preemptive selling advantage by preparing for the sales call, asking the right questions, and presenting a compelling reason why the buyer should focus elsewhere than price.

■ Cutting price is only one way to respond to a price objection.

■ All price objections are not equal.

■ Discounting is real-world but must be done strategically, not randomly.

■ Like discounting, raising prices is real-world, and you can and should do it as needed.

■ When you bid, you have rights unless you choose to cede them to the buyer.

One of my proofreaders said to me, "There is a lot of material in this book. The reader will need to really study this in depth to get the most value from it." Amen. You will need to study this again and again. Price objections will always be there, but they need not defeat you. As I have demonstrated throughout this book, salespeople will often choose the path of least resistance when it comes to price objections. Is this the road you really want to travel, or do you want to take the road less traveled by most salespeople and hold the line on your prices and protect your profit?

Index